WILL THE HONG KONG MODEL SURVIVE?: AN ASSESSMENT 20 YEARS AFTER THE HANDOVER

HEARING

BEFORE THE

CONGRESSIONAL-EXECUTIVE COMMISSION ON CHINA

ONE HUNDRED FIFTEENTH CONGRESS

FIRST SESSION

MAY 3, 2017

Printed for the use of the Congressional-Executive Commission on China

Available via the World Wide Web: http://www.cecc.gov

U.S. GOVERNMENT PUBLISHING OFFICE

26–340 PDF　　　　　WASHINGTON : 2017

For sale by the Superintendent of Documents, U.S. Government Publishing Office
Internet: bookstore.gpo.gov Phone: toll free (866) 512–1800; DC area (202) 512–1800
Fax: (202) 512–2104 Mail: Stop IDCC, Washington, DC 20402–0001

CONTENTS

WILL THE HONG KONG MODEL SURVIVE?: AN ASSESSMENT 20 YEARS AFTER THE HANDOVER

WEDNESDAY, MAY 3, 2017

CONGRESSIONAL-EXECUTIVE
COMMISSION ON CHINA,
Washington, DC.

The hearing was convened, pursuant to notice, at 9:34 a.m., in Room 138, Dirksen Senate Office Building, Hon. Marco Rubio, Chairman, presiding.

Also present: Cochairman Christopher Smith; Senators Steve Daines, Angus King, and Tom Cotton.

OPENING STATEMENT OF HON. MARCO RUBIO, A U.S. SENATOR FROM FLORIDA; CHAIRMAN, CONGRESSIONAL-EXECUTIVE COMMISSION ON CHINA

Chairman RUBIO. All right, good morning. Good morning. This is a hearing of the Congressional-Executive Commission on China. The title of the hearing is "Will the Hong Kong Model Survive?: An Assessment 20 Years After the Handover."

We are going to have two panels testifying today. The first panel will feature the Right Honorable Lord Patten of Barnes, Christopher Patten, testifying via video link from London.

Lord Patten, in addition to serving in the House of Lords, was the last British governor of Hong Kong and oversaw the transfer to China 20 years ago this July.

The second panel will include Joshua Wong from the Umbrella Movement, its leader, now the secretary-general of the new Hong Kong political party Demosistō.

Demosistō? Did I pronounce that? Great.

Martin Lee, barrister, founding chairman of the Democratic Party of Hong Kong, former member of the Drafting Committee for the Basic Law and former member of the Legislative Council of Hong Kong from 1985 through 2008.

Lam Wing Kee, founder, Causeway Bay Books, one of the five forcibly disappeared Hong Kong booksellers.

And Ellen Bork, a writer whose work on democracy and human rights as a priority in American foreign policy, has appeared in the Wall Street Journal, the Washington Post, and the Financial Times, among other publications.

I would also note that translating for Mr. Lam is Ms. Mak Yinting, a journalist and veteran of the Hong Kong Journalists Association, the territory's leading defender of press freedom.

As has already been noted, today's hearing is timely, given the 20th anniversary this July of the British handover of Hong Kong. As we rewatch film footage and commentary of that historic day, we cannot help but take note of the pageantry, the raising and lowering of flags, the solemn handshakes, the national anthems.

Many observers describe the handover as signifying the sunset of a once-great colonial power and the ascent of a rising China. But there was and remains far more at stake.

On that day in 1997, Lord Patten, who we will hear from momentarily, spoke of Hong Kong's unshakable destiny, a Hong Kong governed by and for the people of Hong Kong. And it is that destiny that animates today's gathering.

However, in recent years, Beijing has consistently undermined the "one country, two systems" principle and has infringed on the democratic freedoms that the residents of Hong Kong are supposed to be guaranteed under the Sino-British Joint Declaration, which is an international treaty, and Hong Kong's Basic Law.

The rise of localist politicians and activists who call for greater political and legal self-determination for Hong Kong has drawn harsh reprisals from the Chinese and Hong Kong Governments.

The Chinese Government's November 2016 interpretation of Hong Kong's Basic Law effectively prohibited two recently elected Hong Kong legislators from taking office and was viewed as a blow to Hong Kong's judicial independence.

The Hong Kong Government is currently seeking the removal from office of four other pro-democratic legislators all along the same lines.

In March of this year, nine activists were arrested for their participation in the Occupy Central protests in 2014, including two sitting pro-democratic lawmakers. Their arrests came less than 24 hours after the undemocratic "election" of Carrie Lam to serve as Hong Kong's next chief executive, which drew widespread condemnation and accusations of a retaliatory campaign aimed at punishing leaders of the Hong Kong democracy movement and suppressing dissent prior to her taking office.

In late 2015, five Hong Kong-based booksellers, including one of today's witnesses, were disappeared or abducted to mainland China. One of these booksellers, Gui Minhai, a Swedish citizen abducted from Thailand, remains in custody in China where he will mark his 53rd birthday this coming Friday.

The disappearances and abductions of the booksellers and their coerced, "confessions" which were broadcast on Hong Kong television, sent shockwaves through the city and are reflective of a larger, troubling trend in the area of press freedom and freedom of expression.

Today happens to be World Press Freedom Day and it bears mentioning that the recently released Reporters Without Borders index ranking, which ranks countries for their press freedom environment, had Hong Kong slipping four places in a single year.

In February, Senators Cardin and Cotton joined me in introducing the bipartisan Hong Kong Human Rights and Democracy Act, which would renew the United States' historical commitment to Hong Kong at a time when its autonomy is increasingly under assault.

The legislation also establishes punitive measures against government officials in Hong Kong or mainland China who are responsible for suppressing basic freedoms.

Looking ahead, Congress will be closely watching how Hong Kong authorities and the mainland handle the 20th anniversary as well as whether Ms. Lam moves to reintroduce Article 23, widely despised anti-subversion and anti-sedition legislation first proposed in 2002, which triggered massive protests in which half-a-million Hong Kongers took to the streets.

And for all these reasons is why we look forward to today's hearing, because without question there are many layers and complexities to our relationship with China as evidenced by the questions during yesterday's hearing for Governor Branstad to serve as U.S. Ambassador to China.

Despite the multitude of challenges, Hong Kong's future, indeed its destiny, must not be sidelined. China's assault on democratic institutions and human rights is of central importance to the people of Hong Kong and to its status as a free market, economic powerhouse and hub for international trade and investment.

We cannot allow Hong Kong to go the way of Beijing's failed authoritarianism and one-party rule.

At this time, I would turn to Congressman Smith. And I would note that the congressman has another important bill up for markup. At some point, he will have to leave early, but we, as always, are appreciative of his incredible leadership on this commission and on this cause.

[The prepared statement of Senator Rubio appears in the appendix.]

STATEMENT OF HON. CHRISTOPHER SMITH, A U.S. REPRESENTATIVE FROM NEW JERSEY; COCHAIRMAN, CONGRESSIONAL-EXECUTIVE COMMISSION ON CHINA

Representative SMITH. Thank you very much, Mr. Chairman. And I want to thank you for convening this extremely important and timely hearing.

Two-and-a-half years ago, tens of thousands of Hong Kong residents peacefully gathered in the streets, yellow umbrellas in hand, seeking electoral reform and greater democracy.

Joshua Wong was at the forefront of that movement along with Nathan Law and Alex Chow and so many other young student leaders.

The Umbrella Movement was not only composed of students, but included veterans of the democracy movement in Hong Kong, including the incomparable Martin Lee.

It is good to see Joshua and Martin here today, bringing together the generations of advocates committed to Hong Kong's freedom and autonomy.

Joshua Wong and all those associated with the Umbrella Movement have become important symbols of Hong Kong's vitality and its freedoms. They are now part of Hong Kong's unique brand. And any effort to detain, censor, or intimidate them dangers that brand.

Over the past two years, Senator Rubio and I along with other members of the China Commission have introduced the Hong Kong Human Rights and Democracy Act. And we have worked in Congress to maintain the State Department's annual report on Hong Kong.

We have issued strong statements of solidarity with and concern for the political prosecutions of Joshua and other Umbrella Movement leaders, the unprecedented interventions by the Chinese Government in Hong Kong's courts and political affairs, and the abductions of Hong Kong booksellers and other citizens.

We have also discussed the erosion of Hong Kong's autonomy and freedoms with both U.S. and Chinese officials.

I especially want to commend Senator Rubio for his leadership on human rights issues and on Hong Kong. We have worked together closely and I am honored to work with him on this commission. Senator Rubio is a true champion of the globe's oppressed and persecuted.

As long as I have the privilege of serving as chair of the China Commission, the House chair, I promise to continue shining a light on Hong Kong.

Maintaining Hong Kong's autonomy is a critical U.S. interest. The United States also has a clear interest in Beijing abiding by its international agreements in Hong Kong and elsewhere.

The democratic aspirations of the people of Hong Kong cannot be indefinitely suppressed. My colleagues and I promise to stand with Hong Kong and call attention to violations of basic human rights as they have occurred and, sadly, are still occurring.

Through Beijing's increasingly rough oversight of Hong Kong, though it may not be as brutal as that pursued on the mainland, it is no less pernicious. The ultimate goal is eroding Hong Kong's guaranteed freedoms and the rule of law and intimidating those who try to defend them.

This year will be the 20th anniversary of the handover of Hong Kong. And I think it is very important that Lord Christopher Patten will be testifying. He has provided insights to this commission before, always timely and always very, very incisive.

Unfortunately, it seems the territory's autonomy now looks increasingly fragile. Again, all the more reason why we need to hear from him.

We are coming up on another anniversary as well, the 25th anniversary of the Hong Kong Policy Act. At this juncture, we should be examining both the health of the "one country, two systems" model and examining the very assumptions that underline U.S.-Hong Kong relations, what can be done differently, what new priorities should be set.

The Hong Kong Policy Act of 1992 is based on the assumption that freedom, the rule of law, and autonomy promised to Hong Kong would be protected and respected. It was also based on the assumption that time was on the side of freedom, that trade and investment would eventually bring political liberalization and human rights to mainland China.

As Chairman Rubio and I have been saying for some time, one can no longer base U.S. policy on the fantasy that China's future will be more democratic and more open.

Mainland China has become more repressive under Xi Jinping, not less. Prosperity has turned a poor authoritarian country into a rich authoritarian country with predictable results for China's rights defenders, ethnic and religious groups, labor and democracy advocates, foreign businesses, and Hong Kong's autonomy.

Some will argue that the best course of action would be to retreat into a hard realism, recognizing China's interests and spheres of influence to protect U.S. interests.

We could ignore what is happening in Hong Kong and shift responsibility, say, to the British or some undefined international body. I strongly disagree.

We do not need a new realism to govern our China policy. Instead, we need a new idealism, a renewed commitment to democratic ideals, to human rights and the rule of law in ways that compete directly with the Chinese model in Asia, Africa, and elsewhere.

Chinese leaders need to know that the United States stands for freedom of expression, religion, Internet freedom, the rule of law, universal suffrage, an end to torture, and other fundamental human rights.

Again, I want to thank you and would ask unanimous consent that my full statement be made a part of the record.

And I do regret we have a markup at 10 o'clock on the House side. The first bill that is up is my bill on combating human trafficking, so I have to be there to defend it.

So thank you, Mr. Chairman.

[The prepared statement of Representative Smith appears in the appendix.]

Chairman RUBIO. Thank you. Thank you, Congressman. Thank you for your leadership.

And we will proceed here quickly via our videoconference with Lord Patten.

We thank you for joining us today. We look forward to your testimony and our questions. And I am hoping that you can hear us clearly.

Lord PATTEN. I can indeed.

Chairman RUBIO. Well, thank you for joining us today. You are recognized, sir.

STATEMENT OF THE RIGHT HONORABLE LORD PATTEN OF BARNES, CHRISTOPHER PATTEN, 28TH GOVERNOR OF HONG KONG, 1992–1997 (APPEARING LIVE VIA VIDEO TELECONFERENCE)

Lord PATTEN. First of all, I would like to thank you very much indeed for giving me the opportunity of speaking to you again. I spoke to you last in 2014 in November. And we spoke then principally about the extraordinarily moving demonstrations that were taking place in Hong Kong.

Since then, as you have said, we have had two lots of elections which give a peculiarly Chinese meaning to the word "election" and are not quite the democratic events that you, Senator, and I are used to.

I will not go through all that again. I explored those issues at some length in 2014 in relation to the Joint Declaration, the Basic Law, and the International Covenant on Civil and Political Rights. And all that is on the record.

I can go back over it again if you would like, but it is perfectly clear that Hong Kong has not been given what it was promised by the new sovereign power.

Perhaps I can just, by way of introduction, make four or five points.

The first is one I made before, namely that Beijing, the Chinese Communists consistently argue that what happens in Hong Kong is nobody else's affair and that others should avoid interfering. Well, that is not true on two levels and indeed on a third.

On the first level, Hong Kong's autonomy and way of life for 50 years, guaranteed under the Joint Declaration, which is an international treaty between Britain and China in which first Britain undertook that it would deliver some things to the people of Hong Kong and report on that to China.

And today, the situation is reversed. China is supposed to keep its word to the people of Hong Kong and Britain has every right to interfere in that and argue about whether that has actually happened.

Now, whether or not China keeps its word on the Joint Declaration over time is plainly a matter of considerable interest, which is the second reason why we have to be concerned, to the rest of the international community. Because if China breaks its word over the Joint Declaration and, by extension, the International Covenant and the Basic Law, if China breaks its word on those things, where do we trust it on other international agreements?

And the third point is a straightforward one about Hong Kong's development. Hong Kong is a huge important international trading and economic hub. And an example of that is that there are 1,200 American companies, or perhaps more now, based in Hong Kong. So it is in America's interest and the international community's interest that Hong Kong should be well-governed and should have a reasonable balance between economic and political freedom.

The other points I would like to make very briefly are these, that most of the people I respect in Hong Kong have argued that there has plainly been an erosion of autonomy and of the rule of law over the last few years, direct attacks on autonomy with the abductions that you referred to, and most recently the abduction of a billionaire who was plainly a bag carrier for some of the wealthiest members of the Chinese leadership in Beijing.

There has been pressure on the independence of the judiciary, which I suppose the most outrageous example of that was an intervention by the National People's Congress in a case which was already before the Hong Kong courts and was being properly dealt with.

Third, there are real worries about pressure on the institutional and academic autonomy of universities. I think the view on the part of the Chinese Communist Party is that the democracy movement came out of students and came out of universities, particularly from law faculties, which has encouraged them, the Joint Liaison Office in Hong Kong and others, to interfere in university autonomy.

And freedom of speech, as you said, continues to be a problem. We have not had anything as outrageous as the appalling machete attack on a very brave journalist, Kevin Lau, in the early part of

2014. But there is still the sense of financial and physical intimidation of the press.

The other points I just wanted to make very briefly are, first of all, we have seen, partly because any dialogue with the democracy movement and with young people and with not-so-young people in Hong Kong, any dialogue has been cut off. I think it is not unfair to say that Carrie Lam did not give the impression when she was talking to the students of being very interested in what they had to say.

And I think as a consequence of that, we have seen what I believe to be an unwise development of what is called, politely, localism, the attempt to argue the case for Hong Kong's not just autonomy within China, but for Hong Kong's independence.

And I think a lot of people who are totally supportive as I am of greater progress toward democracy, of standing up for the rule of law, are very, very doubtful about the wisdom of arguing for Hong Kong to have independence as a sovereign state. I simply think that that plays to the hardliners in Beijing. And I do not think it has been terribly wise.

The last points I want to make are there. There is a lot of talk, not least on the part of political scientists, distinguished geopolitical experts like Graham Allison in the United States, about what they call the Thucydides Trap, about the almost inevitable way in which, or they say the inevitable way in which great powers are pushed into dealing aggressively with powers that are on the rise. And that obviously is a backdrop in some respects to the way we handle China in the next few years.

But the way we handle China in the next few years will largely depend on the way that China handles us and the way that China handles its responsibilities. And I think that Hong Kong, to that extent, exemplifies some of the biggest issues that we will face in the century ahead, how China takes its part in the international community, how we balance economic and political freedom, how China copes with its regional relationships.

Now, if China cannot even handle the reasonable democratic aspirations, as it promised to do of people in Hong Kong, it does not give one a huge amount of confidence in its ability to handle wider issues.

We are told that President Xi Jinping may well be going to Hong Kong at the beginning of July to swear-in Carrie Lam and to celebrate the 20th anniversary of the handover of Hong Kong to China.

I hope that if that is true he takes the opportunity to reassure people in Hong Kong that China still stands foursquare behind what it promised back in 1984 and 1985 and later and that he, like Deng Xiaoping, believes that people in Hong Kong are perfectly capable of running their own affairs. It was a very important remark that Deng Xiaoping made back in 1984 to set the minds and hearts of people in Hong Kong at rest.

Well, I have to say, though I think that there is much good that is still happening in Hong Kong, people's minds and hearts are not exactly at rest at the moment.

[The prepared statement of Lord Patten appears in the appendix.]

Chairman RUBIO. We thank you for your testimony.

And I know that you are pressed on time. And we have a substantial time difference. So I will be brief unless any of the other members of the commission appear during your time on our video screen.

And I think you have touched on this already. But how would you assess the British and Chinese Governments with regard to fulfilling their respective obligations under the Joint Declaration?

As you looked 20 years into the future, is this what you thought it would look like? Is this what you had envisioned from both sides 20 years ago?

Or if someone had told you this is the way it was going to look like 20 years later, how would you have felt 20 years ago?

Lord PATTEN. I would have been pleased that the worst that some people anticipated did not happen. There are many, Milton Friedman was one, who thought that "one country, two systems" was impossible. There were others who thought that, for example, even I would be leaving in a helicopter from the ballroom roof in Government House and that sooner or later there would be violence in Hong Kong. And that has not happened, though there has occasionally been some pretty rough policing.

When I was in Hong Kong, we would occasionally have a few hundred people demonstrating. It has been rather different from that.

But there has been, I think, a steady and growing erosion as Anson Chan and as Martin Lee and others have said of Hong Kong's autonomy. And I think that is much to be regretted. And Hong Kong and China will be the losers from that.

I do not want to exaggerate and I have never set myself up as a day-to-day commentator on everything that goes wrong in Hong Kong.

The Taiwanese, of course, not least because "one country, two systems" was designed for them as well, keep a very beady eye on things and have suggested that there have been 169 breaches of the Joint Declaration. Well, I would not say that myself.

What I would say is that the British Government has not always been, and let me choose my words very carefully, has not always been very robust in drawing attention to breaches, whether large or small, of the undertakings, both the letter and the spirit, made by China. And I rather regret that.

The House of Commons Select Committee on Foreign Affairs did produce itself quite a robust report in 2015 having been banned from going to Hong Kong by the Chinese authorities.

I just hope that we will speak out, the British Government will speak out rather more loudly over the coming months and years. I have always felt that we, and I blame myself a bit, but I blame British Governments over a long period of time, I always felt that we let down the generation before Joshua Wong, his parents' generation. And I hope that we do not let down Joshua Wong's generation as well.

Because the most exciting and important thing I think to have happened is there remains in Hong Kong a sense of citizenship in a free society, which is exemplified by the brave way in which Joshua and his colleagues have behaved.

Chairman RUBIO. I believe Senator Daines, who happened to have lived in Hong Kong at the time when you were governor, he says it was very well run. [Laughter.]

But I wanted to give him an opportunity to speak to you across the Atlantic.

Senator DAINES. Governor Patten?

Lord PATTEN. Hello.

Senator DAINES. How are you?

Lord PATTEN. I am very well. I am now running a great university, Oxford University, where we have a lot of Chinese students and a lot of Hong Kong students. And that means that I now enjoy the cut and thrust of the politics of a university rather than the real thing. Universities are sometimes a bit rougher.

Senator DAINES. Well, it is an honor to engage with you today here, Governor Patten.

Just by way of brief introduction, my wife and I moved our family to Guangzhou actually in January 1992. So I watched the transition, and was there as an expat working for Procter & Gamble at the time.

Lord PATTEN. Wow.

Senator DAINES. And in fact, we used to travel back and forth to Hong Kong quite frequently. It was where two of my children were born pre-handover, while you were governor in fact, there at that Matilda Hospital there on top of Victoria Peak.

Lord PATTEN. I know it well.

Senator DAINES. So does my wife. [Laughter.]

But we had a very good experience there, truly.

Lord PATTEN. See, despite some of the criticisms that I have been making, the five years I spent there as governor were the best five years of my life and the best five years of my family's life.

Senator DAINES. Well, I will say, I thought you managed the transition with great honor and dignity at a time there were a lot of people wondering what was going to happen after July 1, 1997.

I was there in Hong Kong on June 30, 1997, and watched the Union Jack come down for the last time. It was kind of a dreary day, like a London day perhaps, when that occurred. But I remember it well.

Lord PATTEN. Certainly like today, it is raining today.

Senator DAINES. Not that it is always dreary in London, but you know what I mean.

I just returned from Hong Kong. In fact, I led a congressional delegation visit to China. We were in Beijing. We were in Hong Kong and we were also in Tokyo. So we had a chance to interact with the LegCo there. We had a chance to have a good conversation with Chief Executive-designate Carrie Lam. And I think it was a constructive conversation.

The change that I have seen, certainly since we moved there in 1992, we returned back to the states shortly after the handover, has been nothing less than profound as I look at Hong Kong as well as the rest of China.

When we moved over there, the Chinese GDP was $500 billion. Today, it is somewhere north of $11 trillion. I believe Hong Kong's percentage of the overall China GDP in 1997 was around 18 percent, I believe.

Lord PATTEN. Yeah.

Senator DAINES. Does that sound about right? And I believe today it is around——

Lord PATTEN. Seventeen, 18, yeah.

Senator DAINES [continuing]. Seventeen to 18 percent. And I think today it is around 3 percent, I believe.

Lord PATTEN. Yes.

Senator DAINES. A function really of just a bigger denominator now. So we have seen the incredible transformation of the economy in China.

My question to you as you have watched this for many, many years, as have I, is, what do you think will be the long-term competitive differentiator between Hong Kong and Shenzhen or Hong Kong and Guangzhou?

Lord PATTEN. The rule of law, above all, which is at the heart of the sense of citizenship, which I think is the standout quality in Hong Kong, which differentiates it from Shanghai or Shenzhen or Guangzhou or the mainland cities. And I think it is an extraordinarily precious sense of Hong Kong-Chinese identity, not just Chinese identity.

What I have often been struck by is the extent to which Chinese officials parrot Deng Xiaoping's expression "one country, two systems," but never actually think through what it means.

Marxists, if such they are, though I think Leninist is a better description, should understand the relationship between economics and politics. And the system in Hong Kong is one in which people have an inherent understanding of the balance between economic and political freedom.

So I do not believe that is going to be stamped out when young men and women like Joshua Wong still feel it as intensely as they do. I certainly do not think it is going to be stamped out. And it will remain a principal reason for Hong Kong's ability to perform successfully so well.

Of course, it is helped by the fact that it is part of the Pearl River Delta economy. Of course, it is helped by the fact that it has both helped to trigger and enjoyed some of the benefits of the extraordinary period of growth in China.

But nobody should underestimate what Hong Kong contributed to that. And I think it is of some relevance that so many Chinese businesses will still come to Hong Kong to arbitrate disputes between them because they can trust the system in Hong Kong, but cannot trust it in mainland China. So I think Hong Kong will continue to have an advantage.

And I would add to that, for a community of its size, and this is something which Hong Kong should be very proud of, for a community of its size, say, 7 million, it is extraordinary that it has 2, maybe 3 of the 50 best universities in the world. It has more universities in the top 50 than Germany or France. That is an outstanding achievement.

And we all know that while there are other reasons for the academy, that it is part of a free society, it also has economic spinoffs which we should not underestimate.

Senator DAINES. Thank you. And I want to make sure I promote you to your proper title as Lord Patten.

Lord PATTEN. Only my wife calls me that. [Laughter.]

Senator DAINES. Well, it was just I still remember you so well as governor. But you recently stated, Lord Patten, that the actions of some Hong Kong democracy activists have actually diluted support for democracy.

Could you elaborate on that? And what advice would you offer these activists?

Lord PATTEN. The advice I would offer them, and I do it with a considerable sense of humility, because they are on the spot, they are taking the risks, they are being much braver than I have ever had to be, let us be clear about that, and the demonstrations in 2014 were an astonishing example to the rest of the world, to all the world, except mainland China where the news was blacked out, they were an extraordinary example of how direct action in promoting democracy can be conducted in a way which is, by and large, nonviolent, particularly unless local triad gangs were let loose on the demonstrators. They behaved, on the whole, with exemplary, peaceful intention.

My worry is that the argument for democracy becomes confused if you start arguing for something which simply is not going to happen.

I cannot think of a large country, of any country which would support Hong Kong becoming an independent, sovereign state. It is just not going to happen.

And what does happen is that people in China are only fed stories about Hong Kong wanting to be independent of the rest of China. They do not know about the struggle for democracy within Hong Kong itself.

I can understand why people feel so frustrated by the lack of democratic progress that they think they have got to go for something bigger. But I think it really does risk reducing support for what is a powerful, a very powerful cause in democracy.

Now, when I was in Hong Kong last November, I made that point to a big meeting of students at Hong Kong University. And they were wonderfully polite; I do not think they agreed with me. I mean, Joshua will know what the figures were, but probably 6(00), 700 people present. And I do not think there was a single question which was supportive of the position I was trying to argue.

But I really did think that I had some skin in this game. And I think that people were likely to listen to me because they knew I was so strongly in favor of the principal objective, which is Hong Kong people running Hong Kong.

Senator DAINES. Lord Patten, we had a conversation with Chief Executive-designate Carrie Lam when I was there a few weeks ago. There were four U.S. Senators and two Members of the House of Representatives that joined that discussion.

One of Carrie Lam's most prominent opponents during the election process was former financial secretary John Tsang who was widely popular——

Lord PATTEN. Yes.

Senator DAINES.—widely popular among the Hong Kong residents. Given his popularity, what is your sense about what his future prospects would be in Hong Kong politics? And how likely do you think Carrie Lam might consider him to be a part of her government?

Lord PATTEN. Well, I think it is uncomfortable for me to make this point. But commendation from the former colonial oppressor may be the kiss of death for some Hong Kong officials. [Laughter.]

I know John Tsang extremely well. He was my private secretary when I was governor. He then represented Hong Kong in London. He is an outstanding public servant and I think that was recognized by the people in Hong Kong who gave him a lead over Carrie Lam of, I think, something like 30 percent. I mean, he had a huge lead in the opinion polls.

I guess he got the thumbs down from the ayatollahs because he counseled on the case for dialogue with the democracy activists whereas Carrie Lam did not seem to think that they needed to be talked to at all. So I think that probably, as far as Beijing was concerned, sank his chances.

But Hong Kong, of course, has a huge amount of talent, not least in the public service. But the talent pool is not so overflowing that you could ignore people like John Tsang. And I hope he will continue to have an active role in the public life of Hong Kong.

But I repeat: I am certainly not going to write him any references because that would sink his chances like a dose of the plague. [Laughter.]

Senator DAINES. Final question for you, Lord Patten. As you look at the relationship between the United States and Hong Kong, what opportunities do you see for greater economic and perhaps political engagement between the United States and Hong Kong?

Lord PATTEN. Well, I want to make one point very strongly. When I was governor of Hong Kong, I had a huge amount of support from the State Department, from senators and congressmen and, which was particularly gratifying, huge support from the American business community.

I think I can say that I had more support from the American business community than I had from any other, and that includes my own nationality.

And there seemed to be a more instinctive understanding of two things. First of all, of the relationship between prosperity and all the freedoms that we take for granted in our democracies. That was important.

And second, I think there was a much smaller, slighter inclination, though it exists a bit everywhere, a much smaller inclination to think that the only way you can do business with China is by kowtowing to China. I think it is complete dribble.

When you actually look at runs of figures, it looks pretty obvious that the Chinese do business on the same basis as everyone else. They try to get the best deal they can at the best price. And I suppose we should not blame them if they take advantage of the fact that a lot of Western governments and even companies seem to think that in order to get a deal or get business you have to bend the knee to Chinese politicians. And I simply do not think it is true.

So I got a huge amount of support from the American business community and American politicians. And I think that continuing to provide that support is very important. I think it is in America's interests as well as Hong Kong's.

And I think that the more the American administration, American politicians make it clear that a very good litmus test of how we all think China might behave in the next few years is how it behaves in Hong Kong. It is not an unreasonable test to apply. They are bound by international treaties and we should hold them to that.

Senator DAINES. Lord Patten, thank you for your insights. My wife and I were together on our last visit to Hong Kong a few weeks ago. And I will tell you, we had a quiet evening walk in Central, reflecting on the Hong Kong of many, many years. We had our two babies there.

And again, I want to thank you for your leadership and your steady hand of leadership during that transition time as the entire world was watching on July 1, 1997.

Thank you, Lord Patten.

Lord PATTEN. Thank you very much. And I hope your Hong Kong babies have grown up into, I am sure they have, into handsome, successful adults.

Senator DAINES. They are, but I will tell you their Cantonese skills are quite weak. [Laughter.]

Chairman RUBIO. Lord Patten, I have two observations before we thank you for your time.

The first is, if your cousins over here across the Atlantic 241 years ago had not been so rebellious in their revolution, both Senator Daines and I would be members of the "U.S. House of Peers" and he would be Lord Daines and I would be Lord Rubio. [Laughter.]

And this is a joke and I am not suggesting it.

Lord PATTEN. And I might have fetched up as governor of Ohio. [Laughter.]

Chairman RUBIO. Yes, sir. Well, it is like that title "supreme allied commander," it is just such a good title, you know? But "senator" is great.

And the second is, as we look at Hong Kong, the one thing that strikes me is it really, in many ways, is an example of what China can and should be, a greater China.

You know, there is this notion out there that somehow democracy is incompatible with the culture, which is absolutely false.

And the second is, just think, this is one of the greatest civilizations in the history of mankind, which has made extraordinary contributions across millennia. Imagine that, that creativity, that thousands of years of culture and tradition and science and all these contributions that the Chinese people have made to the world was unleashed in an environment where there was political freedom, academic freedom, economic freedom.

It would be an extraordinary contribution to the world. Hong Kong, a small, little sliver of land with a limited population, has done so much. It punches above its weight economically. Imagine if that were true for over a billion people in the mainland and what that could mean.

And so for us, as much as anything else, Hong Kong is and remains, and it is why it is so important to us, an example of the extraordinary contributions that I believe the people of China have an opportunity to make in the 21st century to add to the extraordinary tradition of what they have contributed to the world for thousands of years.

I am personally a huge admirer of the Chinese culture, of the Chinese history, of Chinese civilization and of the contributions they have made to all of mankind. And I am excited about what they are going to be able to do, if only over a billion of their people had both the political and economic freedom to truly fulfill their potential.

And I think Hong Kong is a model of what that could look like if only these conditions were not to be eroded moving forward.

Senator DAINES. Chairman Rubio, if I might.

Chairman RUBIO. Absolutely.

Senator DAINES. Maybe I should just say Lord Rubio.

Chairman RUBIO. I thought you were going to, yeah. [Laughter.]

Senator DAINES. Yeah, Lord Rubio.

Chairman RUBIO. This was a joke and the media is watching. I am not actually suggesting you call us "Lord."

Senator DAINES. And the governor of Ohio here who is now on the—yeah.

Chairman RUBIO. Yes.

Senator DAINES. You know, Marco, you brought up a good point.

And, Lord Patten, you mentioned the rule of law as being one of the primary differentiators for the long-term competitiveness of Hong Kong to prosper and to grow.

The other point that I saw, again, when I was in Hong Kong was freedom. And we have seen the freedom indexes that Heritage puts out that Hong Kong is ranked number one. Of all the nations in the world, Hong Kong is ranked number one.

And that was always such an example to me as a young manager for Procter & Gamble moving from the United States to Asia, to see a rock, a chunk of land there with no natural resources and tremendous prosperity and growth. And it was based on freedom, free markets, free trade.

And it should always be a good role model and a case study for us as we look to the future. Thank you.

Lord PATTEN. I agree with everything you have just said. And I agree with everything that Senator Rubio said before about Chinese civilization.

I would just add one point, that it does seem to me that China faces a serious dilemma. And it should perhaps look to Hong Kong to find ways of dealing with it.

On the one hand, there are those in China who say that unless the party gives up control over more of the economy, it will not grow so fast and sooner or later the party will lose control over the state, and others who say that if the party does give up control over the economy, it will certainly lose control of the state.

And I think China's dilemma is, both those propositions are entirely true. And finding a way through those dilemmas, finding an answer to that paradox, well, you might start by getting Hong Kong right.

Chairman RUBIO. Again, we appreciate very much the time you have taken with us and your willingness to use this video conference to do so.

And let us know when you are back in Ohio. [Laughter.]

Lord Patten, thank you so much. We are really grateful to you.

Lord PATTEN. I meant no disrespect for the admirable governor of Ohio, who I saw debating during your interesting presidential election campaign.

Chairman RUBIO. Yes, I went to a few of those debates myself. [Laughter.]

That is another hearing, another time.

Well, thank you. Thank you so much. We appreciate your time. Thank you.

Lord PATTEN. Thank you very much.

Chairman RUBIO. Alright.

Lord Daines, thank you for being here today. [Laughter.]

We have got to stop the "Lord" thing, we are going to get in trouble.

Alright. So we are going to move on. And we are going to make a special kind of accommodation here if the witnesses are alright.

Joshua Wong needs to be on an airplane to Toronto. Assuming we are still going to get through the hearing, but what I would like to do is recognize him for his testimony.

I would encourage you to be brief so we can get to questions and then we can get you to the airport. I can get you through this hearing, I cannot help you through TSA [Transportation Security Administration]. No one can, to be frank. [Laughter.]

But Joshua, we are grateful that you are here today and we look forward to your testimony. I know I have a number of questions. Some of my colleagues could not be here today, they do have some questions in writing, I believe, and we will get those to you and you will answer them when you have some time.

You are one of the busiest young people I have ever met in my life. You must have a lot of frequent flyer miles on your airline as well.

But thank you, Joshua, for being here. We are honored you are here.

Mr. WONG. Alright. Can you turn the mic? The echo sounds, is it possible to turn it——

Chairman RUBIO. That is just for effect to make it more powerful. [Laughter.]

Mr. WONG. Alright.

Chairman RUBIO. No, I am kidding. I am joking. We will figure that out.

Mr. WONG. Alright. Still use this?

Senator DAINES. Try Martin's.

Mr. WONG. Testing, testing. Yeah, I think.

Senator DAINES. Try Martin's. Can you move Martin's over?

Chairman RUBIO. Let us slide over Martin's.

Mr. WONG. Hello? Yeah?

Chairman RUBIO. Yeah, that one works well.

We also have an autotune one which changes your voice a little bit. [Laughter.]

Mr. WONG. Alright.

Chairman RUBIO. There we go.

Mr. WONG. Testing, testing.

STATEMENT OF JOSHUA WONG, UMBRELLA MOVEMENT LEADER AND SECRETARY–GENERAL, DEMOSISTŌ

Mr. WONG. Thank you for the invitation from CECC. This is the first time for me to attend a congressional hearing.

You may have known about Hong Kong's political arrangements as "one country, two systems," but it has now become one country, one-and-a-half systems. And potentially, one country, one system, in the future if conditions continue to worsen.

I was born less than a year before the handover of Hong Kong from the U.K. to China in 1997. Now I am 20 years old.

In the same time, the Hong Kong Government is preparing for its 20th handover anniversary celebration. July 1st will be the first time Xi Jinping visits Hong Kong as the Chinese president.

To pave the way for that, we now face massive political persecution while the government intends to disqualify democratically lawmakers in the oppositional camps, including the core Umbrella Movement student leader, Nathan Law, who was elected last year as the youngest-ever legislator at the age of 23.

Unfortunately, Hong Kong remains far away from democracy after the Umbrella Movement.

Some people think it is a failure because we cannot achieve the goal of universal suffrage. But I am here to tell you guys today that the spirit of the Umbrella Movement is in the hearts of Hong Kong people.

That is why I have been trying to get more support at the international level by strengthening our collaboration around the world.

I am glad to see the reintroduction of the Hong Kong Human Rights and Democracy Act by Senators Rubio, Cotton, and Cardin. Bipartisan support for the bill is proof that protecting Hong Kong's political rights, freedom, and autonomy can be and ought to be a consensus across the political spectrum.

That is why I hope the legislation ensures those who have participated in non-violent assembly in Hong Kong would not be denied American visas on the basis of their criminal record.

Alex Chow, who is in the audience this morning, is another core Umbrella Movement student leader. He was found guilty last July for participating in unlawful assembly, sentenced to three weeks of imprisonment with one year of suspension.

Because of Alex's criminal record, he has faced significant barriers in obtaining a student visa last year for his master's degree in London. He was recently accepted for Ph.D. study at U.C. Berkeley this coming August, which means he will soon apply for a U.S. student visa. And I cannot stress the importance for this legislation for many of those like Alex who may potentially face difficulties entering free countries.

China's suspension against us is helped by its growing regional domination. Last year, I was invited by a Thai university, but was not allowed to enter the country and locked for 12 hours in a detention cell.

My request to contact a lawyer or at least notify my family in Hong Kong were both rejected. I was very worried to be the next

Gui Minhai, one of the five booksellers abducted from Thailand to China.

Luckily, I was finally released. But the Thai Government later said that I will be forever banned to enter the country at request by China.

If the Hong Kong Human Rights and Democracy Act passes, the proposed legislation, I hope it will place human rights and democracy at the center of future American policy toward Hong Kong. It will send a strong signal to Beijing that, as a world leader, the beliefs of the United States are just as important to protect political freedom in Hong Kong as it is to protect economic freedom.

The support of the proposed legislation is also in the American interests. Hong Kong is home to around 85,000 U.S. citizens and 1,400 U.S. companies. Two-way Hong Kong and U.S. trade was around 42 billion U.S. dollars last year. And most American media outlets, including CNN, the Wall Street Journal, and Time magazine have established an Asian office in Hong Kong.

This is all evidence that, despite all the difficulties it is facing, Hong Kong remains the freest city under Chinese administration.

In conclusion, I hope Democrats and Republicans alike can work together to defend the fundamental human rights value that they share. We Hong Kongers will continue to fight, hear our heart, against the Communist regime for the day to come for us with democracy and to exercise the right of self-determination.

I started to fight for democracy six years ago when I was 14 years old. The father of Hong Kong's democracy sits next to me, Martin Lee. He is turning 79 years old this year. After four decades of struggle, I wonder, if I come to the age of 79, will I be able to see democracy?

My aspiration and our generation's challenge is to ensure that Hong Kong continues as the beacon of human rights and freedom for China and the world.

To sum up, today the authoritarian regime dominates my generation's future. But the day will come when we decide our future. No matter what happens to the protest movement, we will claim that democracy belongs to us and continue our fight because time is on our side.

Thank you.

[The prepared statement of Mr. Wong appears in the appendix.]

Chairman RUBIO. Thank you, Joshua.

Thank you. We are grateful that you are here, and have tremendous admiration for your advocacy. And I have often spoken about you to university students that I teach at Florida International University and in other places as an example of political engagement under quite difficult circumstances.

We take, sometimes I should say, our freedoms for granted here in the United States because we have extraordinary freedoms. But we are reminded through you and others that there are incredible people around the world that are confronting this, as some of the panelists have as well.

And again, I know you need to get to Canada, so I wanted to ask you a couple of questions.

First, can you tell us how the Hong Kong Government's legal actions against democracy advocates and members of the opposition have influenced your thinking about the future of Hong Kong's democracy movement?

Mr. WONG. Last year, September, was the Legislative Council election. Four newly elected legislators upholding civil disobedience entered the Legislative Council from the civil society. And later, the government just issued a court case to four of them, including two others advocating Hong Kong independence.

Even if I am not the one advocating Hong Kong independence, but disqualifying the democratically elected legislators just proves that the Chinese and Hong Kong Governments will try to override the judicial independence and rule of law in Hong Kong. And it is totally not respectful to the current election system.

And at the same time, political persecutions happen and also prove the hard line of President Xi. It is just following by newly elected chief executive Carrie Lam.

After the 26th of March, the election day of the chief executive— the day after—the Hong Kong Government just arrested and prosecuted nine Umbrella Movement leaders. And it is just proof that in the future it will not be an easy time for us to fight for democracy.

At the same time, the 3rd of July will be another court case and a trial for many to face. And the sentence is contempt of court. And in the worst case, I may be sent to prison for a few months or even a few years.

But I will say that now, in fact, the fight for democracy is a long-term battle. In the last battle three years ago in the Umbrella Movement, even we cannot achieve a concrete political system reform, but at least we raised a new generation's political awareness and keep the international community's eyes on Hong Kong.

That is why in this long-term battle, the new generation is ready for this fight until the day we get back democracy.

Chairman RUBIO. Well, explain to me, in your view, what does self-determination for Hong Kong mean?

Mr. WONG. Self-determination to Hong Kong means that the political system, political status, and future constitutional arrangement of Hong Kong should be decided by Hong Kong people.

According to the Sino Joint Declaration, it is proof that Hong Kong can implement "one country, two systems" from 1997 to 2047 under the 50 years unchanged policy framework. After 2047, I will be 51 years old. At that moment, I am not sure whether Hong Kong will turn to be one country, one-and-a-half systems or in a worse case, one country, one system.

And what we hope is to let people realize that it is time for Hong Kong people to rule Hong Kong. And it is time for Hong Kong people to determine their own future.

Chairman RUBIO. Finally, what recommendations, and you touched on it a little bit when you talked about the hope that we could come together in a bipartisan way on some of these issues, do you have any recommendations on things we can do, whether it is this commission, the Congress, President Trump's administration, on what we can do here from the U.S. Government side to promote continued protections in Hong Kong for democracy and human rights and the rule of law? What is the best thing we can be doing?

Mr. WONG. I hope the Hong Kong issue can get a higher priority in the political agenda of the United States toward China policy.

We know that the South China Sea, Taiwan issue or others are always the main issues or the incidents that we need to tackle or face. But the fact is, I believe supporting democracy in Hong Kong just relies totally on the international treaty, Sino-British Joint Declaration.

So what I hope is, in the future, supporting democracy in Hong Kong should be a bipartisan consensus. And I believe it is also an achievable goal for the international civil society.

In the future, apart from having op-eds, press release statements before the 1st of July, to let people realize that while Xi Jinping has to approve everything that is under his control, we will still organize and hold large-scale demonstrations in Hong Kong to let him and the Chinese Government know that we are still continuing our fight to democracy.

And at the same time, we just hope people around the world, especially in the international community, no matter senator or congressman, apart from op-eds and press releases, we hope will have the possibility to figure out a chance of organizing a delegation to Hong Kong and also pushing forward the Hong Kong Human Rights and Democracy Act.

In the global effort, the international community can realize that supporting Hong Kong democracy is the only gateway or the window for us to push forward on the Chinese Communist regime to respect human rights, democracy, and rule of law.

That is why, according to the U.S. business interests which care about the stability and prosperity of Hong Kong, according to what I have mentioned about the citizens and U.S. companies in Hong Kong, I hope in the future the new administration can also take Hong Kong as a higher priority agenda.

Chairman RUBIO. And I just want you to know that both in our private meeting and yesterday at our hearing, we have discussed with the president's nominee to be Ambassador to Beijing, Governor Branstad of Iowa, the importance of Hong Kong and of your cause.

And my hope is that we can facilitate an opportunity for you and members of your political party to meet with him, if not here before he leaves, certainly once confirmed by the Senate.

My final question for you, Mr. Wong is, I know that last week several Legislative Council members had been targeted for removal, but several of the party members were arrested last week. Can you update us on their status.

Mr. WONG. The disqualification of the legislators' court case was issued in May, which means that a few weeks later, maybe two or three weeks later, we will know the results, including the Umbrella Movement student leader, Nathan Law, the youngest lawmaker in my hometown, whether they can still keep their seat in the Legislative Council.

In the worst case, due to the current legal system in Hong Kong, if those legislators lose their court case, they need to pay the legal fees of the government side worth 3 million. So it will have the chance of facing bankruptcy for Nathan Law and other legislators.

That is why it is time for us to face the prosecution and also the disqualification of legislators.

Chairman RUBIO. Were several members of your political party arrested last week? Where are they now?

Mr. WONG. Yes. At the same time on Friday, two days later, the political movement activists, including two party members from my political party, Demosistō, Ivan Lam and Derek Lam, they will face a trial in the courts due to their participation in the assembly last November against the reinterpretation of the Basic Law from the National People's Congress.

Chairman RUBIO. But of the ones that were—how many were arrested last week?

Mr. WONG. Nine.

Chairman RUBIO. Nine.

Mr. WONG. Yes.

Chairman RUBIO. Of the nine that were arrested, do any remain in custody?

Mr. WONG. They still get a chance to get bail and now they will wait. They are waiting to go to the courts on Friday and to face a trial.

Chairman RUBIO. But they are still in jail right now?

Mr. WONG. No.

Chairman RUBIO. They are out.

Mr. WONG. They are not in jail.

Chairman RUBIO. Oh, they are not. They were released.

Mr. WONG. Yes, they were released and got a court bail.

Chairman RUBIO. And now they are awaiting trial.

Mr. WONG. Yes, awaiting the trial.

Chairman RUBIO. Well, we appreciate very much, Mr. Wong, your being here today. We have seen you quite a bit in the last few months. I encourage you to continue to do what you are doing. Know that this commission, my office, the members remain at your disposal to continue to highlight your cause and the greater cause of democracy and rule of law in Hong Kong. And I wish you continued success, both on your trip now and as you work your way through.

Which airport are you going through, Reagan or Dulles?

Mr. WONG. I am not sure, I need to check my ticket. Sorry for that.

Chairman RUBIO. Yes. Maybe we should not announce which one you are going to. [Laughter.]

Mr. WONG. Yes, thank you.

Chairman RUBIO. He is leaving from Baltimore. [Laughter.]

So anyway, Mr. Wong, thank you very much for coming and we look forward to continuing to talk to you more and more about this in the weeks and months to come.

Mr. WONG. Thank you. Yes, I appreciate it. And thank you to the CECC in their previous few years, especially since the Umbrella Movement, continuing to put effort to support universal suffrage, democracy, and the democratic camps in Hong Kong.

Chairman RUBIO. Well, we are just getting started. We are going to continue to press on the case. So we thank you so much.

Mr. WONG. Yes, it is a long-term battle. Thank you.

Chairman RUBIO. We are going to move on now to our panel. And again, thank you for your indulgence because of the flight situation.

So, Mr. Lee, I guess we will begin with you. And we thank you for being here and thank you for letting us use your microphone.

STATEMENT OF MARTIN LEE, BARRISTER; FOUNDING CHAIRMAN, DEMOCRATIC PARTY OF HONG KONG; FORMER MEMBER, DRAFTING COMMITTEE FOR THE BASIC LAW; AND FORMER MEMBER, LEGISLATIVE COUNCIL OF HONG KONG (1985–2008)

Mr. LEE. Thank you, Mr. Chairman. Thank you for calling me as an expert witness.

I remember the first testimony I gave to Congress was 1989, shortly after the massacre in Tiananmen Square. In a way, Hong Kong has been a miracle, because it is a tiny dot at the coast of China, and yet, even today, according to Lord Patten, with whom I agree, there is still the rule of law which separates Hong Kong from every other Chinese city. But that rule of law is now under threat, more than ever before.

Chinese leaders have been asking our courts to cooperate with the government. And in June 2014, the Chinese state department issued a white paper in seven languages saying that all our judges are administrators, like other civil servants; and therefore, in trying cases, they must safeguard China's sovereignty, security, and development interests.

The judges are extremely worried. Judges are human beings. You cannot expect judges alone to defend the rule of law without giving them the support of the community via democracy.

And democracy has been delayed; delayed many times already. Under the Basic Law, our mini constitution, we were supposed to have full democracy after 10 years of the handover. This is now almost 20 years after the handover, still I cannot tell you when we will have genuine democracy.

So Hong Kong is undergoing a very serious threat at the moment. That is why we are here. We are here to tell the world that things are going wrong. They are going wrong because China has not been honoring her obligations under the Sino-British Joint Declaration promising us democracy and the rule of law.

Now, we have a window of opportunity because Mr. Xi Jinping will come to Hong Kong on July 1 to celebrate the 20th anniversary of Hong Kong going back to China. Mr. Xi must be told, politely, of course, but firmly, that the eyes of the world are on China, the eyes of the world are on Hong Kong.

I think the administration here must realize that in dealing with China and hopefully making treaties with China over many issues, your administration must bear in mind that Hong Kong is now part of China. And if China can break an international agreement over Hong Kong with impunity, how much confidence can you have over new treaties to be made with China over other issues?

So when I look at Hong Kong's future, I have confidence, in particular, because of the young leaders, like Joshua Wong and others. They have been fighting for democracy. They are now in trouble. They are prepared to pay the price for it.

Of course, I would appeal to you, Mr. Chairman and your colleagues, to think of Hong Kong whenever you are dealing with China.

I thank you for giving the Hong Kong people the support over my years of fighting for democracy in Hong Kong. I hope you will continue to give encouragement to the young leaders because they need your support more than we did, because the threat on Hong Kong's freedoms and the rule of law is now greater than ever before.

But I must take a little time to thank your staff members. In fact, I do not understand why you want me to be an expert; they are experts on China and Hong Kong.

And I thank you for the attention that, Mr. Chairman, you and your colleagues have continued to give to Hong Kong. And may the Hong Kong miracle continue. Thank you.

Chairman RUBIO. Thank you. We, too, are very proud of our staff and of the work that they do. And I appreciate your thanks.

I do not require any thanks. I was raised in a community of people that lost their freedom, which makes me incredibly sensitive to people all over the world who are losing theirs.

And with that, I turn to Mr. Lam for his testimony.

And I thank you as well for being here. Your case and your work is inspiring to all of us.

[The prepared statement of Mr. Lee appears in the appendix.]

STATEMENT OF LAM WING KEE, FOUNDER, CAUSEWAY BAY BOOKS, ONE OF FIVE VICTIMS OF THE FORCED DISAPPERANCES OF HONG KONG BOOKSELLERS

Ms. MAK [Interpreter]. Hi, I am Mak. Thank you, Mr. Chairman. I am Mak, a veteran journalist for over three decades and have been a witness to the erosion of Hong Kong's press freedom after the handover.

The abduction of Mr. Lam Wing Kee, which I am going to translate for, is a case in point.

The interference of the Chinese Government and its agents to press freedom in Hong Kong has changed from indirect to direct. Now is the time for us to listen to Lam Wing Kee in his own words. Lam.

Mr. LAM. [Through interpreter.] Between October and December 2015, the disappearance of five persons of Causeway Bay Books in Hong Kong was investigated and confirmed by the Hong Kong media. The five were suspected to have been arrested or abducted by the Chinese Government.

On October 17, Gui Minhai, a shareholder, was taken away from an apartment in Pattaya, Thailand by men.

Lui Bo, another shareholder, was arrested by public security people in Shenzhen, China while having lunch in a restaurant.

Cheung Jinping, an employee, was taken away from his home in Dongguan, China by armed policemen on the 23rd of October.

I, myself, an employee, was detained by customs when I entered Shenzhen via the Lowu border on October 24 and secretly taken to Ningbo the next day. Lee Bo, also a shareholder, was abducted on December 30 in a warehouse parking lot in Chai Wan and forcibly taken across the border to the mainland of China by nine persons.

Prior to the Causeway Bay Books incident, an elderly publisher named Yao Wentian, publisher of Morning Bell Press in Hong Kong, was lured to Shenzhen and arrested in October 2013, because he had been preparing to publish a book that was critical of Xi Jinping.

In May 2015, he was charged for the crime of smuggling general cargo and sentenced to imprisonment of 10 years by the Shenzhen Intermediary People's Court.

The owner, Wang Jianmin, and editor, Guo Zhongxiao, of another company that published the magazines New Way Monthly and Multiple Face, were consecutively arrested in their homes in Shenzhen. Two years later, they were sentenced to imprisonment of five years, three months and two years, three months, respectively.

This string of events demonstrates not only brutal intervention in the freedom of expression in Hong Kong by the Chinese Government, but also how increasingly unscrupulous they are. They have arrested people at will with utter disregard for the law.

According to Article 22 of the Basic Law, no department of the Central People's Government and no province, autonomous region or municipality directly under the central government may interfere in the affairs which the Hong Kong special administrator administers on his own in accordance with the Basic Law.

According to Article 27 of the Basic Law, Hong Kong residents shall have freedom of speech, of the press, and of publication.

According to Article 34 of the Basic Law, Hong Kong residents shall have the right to engage in literary and artistic creation and other cultural activities.

From the events described, it can be seen that at least the above three articles of the Basic Law have been violated by the Chinese Government. Undoubtedly, the Chinese Government has violated legal provisions and seriously contravened its promise of allowing a high degree of autonomy to Hong Kong people.

Chairman RUBIO. If I may for just one second, Mr. Lam.

If you will translate for me so he will understand.

Here is our predicament. We only have you until 11:30. The Senate, as democracy works, has called a vote. And if I leave, the commission has to stop.

Here is what I would propose, if this is possible. I would need to adjourn for five minutes so I can go to the floor, vote and come back. We can submit the entirety of the testimony into the record so he does not have to sit and read.

And when I return, we can get to Ms. Bork and then to our questions so that I can still get you out by 11:30. But if there were other members here, we could trade. I am the only one here. So if I leave, apparently everything stops.

And I am truly apologetic. I do not control the vote schedules. So if this is alright with Mr. Lam. Is that fine?

Mr. LAM. Alright.

Chairman RUBIO. So it will probably take me about seven minutes, maybe eight if there are a lot of reporters in the hallway and I have to fight my way through them, and I will be back here so we can continue because I do want to get to Ms. Bork and I want to get to our questions.

It is important that the answers get on the record because we use this with our colleagues to advocate policy.

So we are going to stand for a quick recess of no more than 10 minutes while I vote and return.

[Whereupon, at 10:53 a.m. the hearing was recessed and resumed back on the record at 11:08 a.m.]

Chairman RUBIO. Alright, thank you for your indulgence.

So I think we have a little bit of time left to finish the conclusion in English of Mr. Lam's testimony, then we can get to Ms. Bork and we can get to our questions.

I do not believe there will be any other votes in the next 30, 45 minutes.

Ms. MAK. Alright. Let me just read out the statement by Mr. Lam.

Being a victim in the Causeway Bay Books incident, I was illegally detained at first in Ningbo and then in Shaoguan for eight months. During that period, I was subjected to intimidating interrogation and was deprived of the rights to hire a solicitor and to inform my family.

They also intended to force me into becoming an accomplice in carrying out continuous surveillance on the people of Hong Kong and the mainland of China.

I earnestly urge the U.S. Government and Members of the Congress to pay heed to the notion of universal values, safeguard justice and human rights, freedom and democracy and exert pressure on the Chinese Government to release Gui Minhai, publisher of Mighty Current publishing, and Mr. Lee Ming-che, human rights advocate of Taiwan, who has been detained by the Chinese Government recently.

Mr. Gui Minhai is the only person of the Causeway Bay Books incident still detained. Like myself, he was also forced to confess on television. His daughter, Angela Gui, had testified before this same commission last year.

It would be most helpful if this commission can urge President Trump to bring attention to the cases of Mr. Gui and Mr. Lee when he visits China and President Xi Jinping later this year.

In regard to the fact that Mr. Gui is a Swedish citizen and Mr. Lee Bo is a British citizen, China's foreign minister, Wang Yi, stated that they are first and foremost Chinese. And in fact, he is claiming that, regardless of their citizenship, the Chinese Government has the right to assert its control over all ethnic Chinese in the world.

In respect of the Chinese Government's increasingly severe intervention in Hong Kong's administration, I appeal to the U.S. Congressional-Executive Commission on China to implement stipulations in the U.S.-Hong Kong Policy Act of 1992 as soon as possible to compel the Chinese Government to fulfill its assurance to Hong Kong people. Otherwise, Hong Kong would degenerate into a second-rate Chinese city way before year 2047.

Now I would like to speak on behalf of Hong Kong Journalists Association to say it is a critical time for freedom of the press and publishing to survive.

We will continue our fight in Hong Kong. I would like to urge the commission to act now to back journalists, publishers, and freedom of information in Hong Kong. And thank you for your concern and support.

Chairman RUBIO. Thank you so much.

Ms. Bork, thank you for your patience. And thank you for being here.

[The prepared statement of Mr. Lam appears in the appendix.]

STATEMENT OF ELLEN BORK, AUTHOR

Ms. BORK. Not at all. Thank you for inviting me and giving me this opportunity to underscore what the people of Hong Kong are saying through elected representatives and the leaders of their democracy movement.

The last time Congress took a really serious, in-depth look at policy and making law in Hong Kong was well over 25 years ago. A lot of things have changed since then.

We have heard about the steady erosion of its autonomy and assaults on its civil liberties, interference in the courts.

A good discussion could be had about whether there really was a meeting of the minds between Great Britain and China at the time. In any case, I do not think the Joint Declaration and its implementing legislation, which was passed by the National People's Congress, does justice to the people of Hong Kong.

Hong Kong's freedom depends mostly on the support of the international community. That support has been, I think, quite strong in some ways, but too deferential to the arrangements that were written by China or agreed to by China with an eye toward keeping China's control through its control of the chief executive, giving it the right to reinterpret law and not allowing full democracy, as we have seen several times over the last few years.

The arrangements that were made, and the U.S. policy based on them, were aspirational. Today, I think we have to take a much different approach to see what China is doing in Hong Kong and also how Hong Kong relates to its more assertive role around the world in challenging democratic norms.

We hoped that Hong Kong would exist as an island in the midst of a huge autocratic system. That was unrealistic. If we want to protect Hong Kong, we have to look at China's role more broadly in undermining democratic norms around the world.

That is why I think the Hong Kong Democracy and Human Rights Act is extremely important. It changes the outlook that Congress is taking, no longer hoping that Beijing will recognize its interest in Hong Kong's survival.

Americans, I think, tend to project optimism onto other countries. We hope to find common ground and support for democracy, even in unlikely places, that is among the leaders of the Chinese Communist Party. Our Hong Kong policy was really based on that. Now we have to be a little bit hardnosed and realistic.

The existing U.S.-Hong Kong Policy Act does not have much of a penalty, or enforcement. It does not impose consequences for what China has done in Hong Kong. It allows the president to change Hong Kong's status in some aspects of law, but that actually hurts the people of Hong Kong. It does not put the penalty where it belongs, which is on Chinese officials and their proxies who might be taking these steps.

Some of the steps that they are taking are increasingly alarming as we have heard from my fellow witnesses here today.

The most important thing about the Hong Kong Democracy and Human Rights Act is that it responds to interference, that long reach of China into Hong Kong. That is an extremely worrisome development, but it is also not an isolated one.

The party has acted to seize dissidents in other countries. It has acted to repatriate Uyghurs. And frankly, this has gone relatively unopposed. We need to find ways to stand up to that.

Also, we notice the criminalization of dissent, the prosecution of Hong Kong democrats. It is clear the party is going to go after Hong Kong democrats the way they go after dissidents and Uyghurs and, if they could, the Dalai Lama. China, I think, is behind Russia in manipulating the red notices of the Interpol system, but we can see from the way they are beginning to prosecute Hong Kong people that they have that in mind.

The most important thing Congress can do right now is begin to treat Hong Kong as integral to a response to China's assertiveness. Congress should also consider China's assertiveness on democratic values as related to its military assertiveness as well.

As long as the United States does not articulate support for democracy in Hong Kong and in China, I do not think we will be very convincing in our rejection of their aggression elsewhere.

Thank you.

Chairman RUBIO. Thank you.

And are you prepared for questions, Senator?

Senator KING. Sure.

Chairman RUBIO. I will defer to my colleague, Senator King, for the first round of questions.

And you were not here, but Joshua Wong was here a moment ago. He had to leave for Canada, not permanently, just he is receiving an award, so we took his testimony and his questions ahead. But thank you for coming.

Senator KING. Yes, sir.

This is a question for anyone on the panel. I visited Hong Kong some time ago and it was one of the most vital and energetic cities I have ever visited in the world.

My question is, today's hearing and the materials that have been submitted have documented, I think, the diminution of the democratic ideal in Hong Kong. My question is, has that in turn affected the economy, vitality, energy, and forward-looking economy of the city?

Mr. Lee, you want to start?

Mr. LEE. Of course, it is very difficult to translate that in terms of dollars and cents. But it is the effect of the mood of the city and the mood of the people.

Now, at the moment, after almost five years of governorship as it were or stewardship under the outgoing chief executive, Mr. CY Leung, the city, the population there is split. Now, that is a tactic deliberately employed by him and his minders who are in the central government liaison office. That is the Communist people in Hong Kong.

And so when you have got a split community, it is very difficult to get things done. And I think the best person whom I quote is the last president of the Legislative Council in Hong Kong, who, in fact, belonged to their group, but is a very fair person. And he said that unless there is democratic reform in Hong Kong very soon, Hong Kong is ungovernable. And that is from the outgoing or the last president of the Legislative Council.

So the new one, the chief executive-elect who will take office in a couple of months' time, now, Carrie Lam, in fact, before she won the election, said in public that she intends to continue with the policy of her predecessor.

So everything now hinges on the president of China. If he does not intervene and correct this direction that has been going on in Hong Kong for almost 20 years now, then Hong Kong will soon go down the drain. We cannot afford to have another five years of this policy. This policy must be reversed.

Senator KING. Others comment on my observation or question, whether the de-democratization is leading to a diminution of economic activity?

Mr. LEE. As I said, it has to be negative. But of course, I cannot give you dollars and cents at all. Because I remember, before the handover, there was a poll conducted among U.S. businesspeople in Hong Kong asking them, what would cause them to leave Hong Kong after the handover?

There were two things. The environment, if the air is polluted to such an extent, they would rather run away from Hong Kong.

Senator KING. I remember the problem with the air.

Mr. LEE. And the other one is the loss of the rule of law. So that is very important to businesspeople. If they see the rule of law not there, why should they do business in Hong Kong?

But at the moment, the good news is our judges are still holding out. But how long can they last when they are subjected to such pressure from the central authorities?

Senator KING. Ms. Bork, do you have any observations?

Ms. BORK. I do not have numbers, but I do think the question is what kind of economic activity. And as Martin says, whether the rule of law is affecting the way business is done. So I do not have any information on the volume of business.

My sense anecdotally is that people feel the climate not only in freedoms of society has changed, but that the business climate also has changed. But I am honestly not the best person to comment on that.

Senator KING. I think it would be helpful to this commission if either other witnesses or staff could perhaps present some data——

Ms. BORK. Sure.

Senator KING [continuing].——in terms of GDP of the city, employment, population——

Mr. BORK. And corruption.

Senator KING [continuing].——corruption, indicia of activity. What I am trying to get at is, does the change in the governing system translate into a loss of economic opportunity for the residents. That is what I am looking for, so perhaps someone could think about that or our staff. I think that would be very helpful to look at the data and compare it with other areas, Shanghai for example, other areas of China.

I think I am—yes?

Mr. LEE. Can I perhaps have a follow up? And it is this. I entirely agree, figures could help. But one must remember that even if the figures show an improvement, one does not know how much more improvement there would have been——

Senator KING. Sure.

Mr. LEE [continuing].——but for the erosion of the rule of law. But I agree with you, figures would certainly give some guidance.

Senator KING. Right, thank you.

Chairman RUBIO. Senator Cotton, are you prepared or did you want me to ask a question while you get ready?

Senator COTTON. Always prepared.

Chairman RUBIO. Alright, good.

Senator COTTON. I apologize to the witnesses, including the witnesses that had to leave. I was presiding over the Senate, which these two relatively junior Members of the Senate also know is a duty, not an honor. [Laughter.]

So thank you for your patience.

And I do want to thank you all for taking the time to testify today, but, more importantly, for the work you do to inform the world about Beijing's continued encroachments on human rights and basic freedoms in Hong Kong.

This summer, Xi Jinping will mark the 20-year anniversary of Chinese control over Hong Kong with a visit to the city. One cannot be faulted for likening Mr. Xi's impending arrival to Hong Kong to that of a Roman emperor inspecting what he views as conquered lands. Because since his ascendance to power, Xi has accelerated Beijing's campaign to suppress all avenues of dissent in Hong Kong.

First, he has targeted members of Hong Kong civil society to include the most vibrant members of civic life in the city, its publishers, journalists, and students, who now must fear being abducted in the middle of the night.

When Chinese security forces are not conducting cross-border snatch-and-grab missions, they instead rely on Hong Kong Government loyalists to round up opposition figures on false charges.

Suppressing civil society, though, is not enough for Mr. Xi. The specter of Beijing's authoritarianism has now fallen on Hong Kong's legislative branch as well. Last year, China's National People's Congress barred pro-independence legislators from taking their seats in the city's Legislative Council.

The incident only highlights Beijing's view that Hong Kong's independence is a convenient fiction, one that can be swept aside when it feels the need to rule by dictate.

In July, Hong Kong's news chief executive, Ms. Carrie Lam, will take office. While I sincerely hope that Ms. Lam will act as an independent voice to stand for the basic freedom of all Hong Kongers, I certainly am not holding my breath. After all, Ms. Lam was Beijing's preferred candidate in this year's closed-door election by committee.

How far we have come from the "one country, two systems" construct agreed to by Margaret Thatcher in 1984. How far we have come from the fiercely independent government that Lord Patten envisioned when he handed over control of Hong Kong on that rainy night 20 years ago in 1997.

Slowly, but surely, Beijing has revealed that it never intended to honor its promises in Hong Kong. In the mind of the Communist Party leaders, to accept a true Chinese democracy would endanger Communist rule.

I believe Beijing has this exactly backward. Instead of viewing a flourishing and autonomous Hong Kong as a threat, to see it as a shining example of what is possible in China and for the Chinese people. Instead of clinging to a system built on autocratic control and endemic corruption, centralized planning, Beijing should look to Hong Kong as a herald of reform.

But unfortunately, Beijing has not followed that path. Instead, it increasingly resorts to gross human rights violations to quell dissent in Hong Kong. I believe the United States should not quietly accept the state of affairs.

I am pleased to have introduced with Senator Rubio and Senator Cardin the Hong Kong Human Rights and Democracy Act which would require the president to identify and sanction persons responsible for suppressing basic freedoms of journalists, activists, and others in Hong Kong.

Chinese Communist cadres who order the kidnapping and torture of members of Hong Kong civil society should not be allowed to stash their immense wealth in New York high-rises and Malibu beach homes.

Now, some may say these sanctions are harsh or inappropriate for an issue that China deems an internal matter. I do not see that as the case. Hong Kong's autonomy is not a domestic Chinese issue after all, but a matter of Beijing honoring a longstanding international commitment. And if it will breach that commitment, which commitment will it not breach?

Thank you all again for appearing before us today. And I want to turn to an impending question that many of us have on our mind, the accession of Carrie Lam to be the chief executive for Hong Kong.

As you know, she served as Hong Kong's government representative in a two-hour televised debate with the Umbrella Movement leaders over Hong Kong's system of government. Given her history, I would like to ask each of our witnesses, do you believe she is willing or able to engage constructively with Hong Kong's pro-democracy groups, act independently from Beijing, and support rights legally granted to all Hong Kongers?

And I will start from my left and move to my right.

Mr. LEE. First of all, Senator, thank you for co-sponsoring this important bill.

Now, right after her victory, Ms. Carrie Lam actually said that she would engage the democrats and talk about livelihood issues. But she also said on democracy issues, that would have to wait.

Now, the trouble that we find ourselves in today in Hong Kong is because democracy, which was promised, has been delayed again and again. So she must not put democracy on the back burner and expect to work with the democrats.

So the democratic camp and legislators in the democratic camp are not going to talk with her simply on livelihood issues. Of course, that is important, too. But she must start a dialogue with the democratic camp on democracy. Because without it, then the rule of law cannot be guaranteed.

Senator COTTON. Thank you.

Ms. Bork, if you would like to start.

Ms. BORK. I am skeptical about how much a chief executive of Hong Kong can do, mainly because of the system that is set up where, in this case, she is chosen by a small committee of people of largely pro-Beijing sentiments. So I do not think it is sort of entirely up to her.

And I do not think any of the chief executives have had great success, in a way because they are limited by this. They have to represent a people who do not get to pick them, but they are really carrying out, ultimately, Beijing's wishes, certainly on political matters. So I am not optimistic that she has any interest or latitude to advance democracy during her term at all.

Senator COTTON. Mr. Lee.

Mr. LEE. May I just elaborate a little more on that? I think Ms. Bork is entirely right.

I think even if Carrie Lam wants to do good things for Hong Kong, she can only do so if Beijing permits her to do so. She is now the fourth, she will be the fourth chief executive in Hong Kong. And each one of them is actually handpicked by Beijing, because this so-called election committee consists of over 75 percent of their people.

Senator COTTON. Mr. Lam.

Mr. LAM. I am afraid that, in terms of freedom of expression, there might be a threat that this group of freedom of expression may be narrowed down further because of the enactment of the Article 23.

So if such a legislation was enacted, whoever is talking about the independence of Hong Kong, independence of Taiwan, of Tibet, Mongolia, will not be allowed it. And even research in this regard will be limited, so that will hurt the freedom of publications.

And I am worried that the chief executive to be will just follow the wish of mainland China and enact the Article 23 of the Basic Law separately, not in monolithic legislation, but separately, which will limit the freedom of Hong Kong people.

That is all.

Senator COTTON. And one final question that I would like to get your perspective on if you care to share.

Given the recent arrests and crackdowns on pro-democracy activists and lawmakers, many analysts say this is in anticipation of Mr. Xi's visit later this year, do you agree? And if so, do you expect that to intensify in the coming weeks?

Mr. LEE. There are two ways of looking at it. One way is that Mr. Xi certainly would like his visit to be welcomed by the people of Hong Kong.

Now, the other way of looking at it is the Hong Kong administration would like to suppress more demonstrations and free expressions of views in order to let him come to Hong Kong without hearing too many noises. So I do not know what the outcome is.

Now, if Mr. Xi knows what may happen in Hong Kong, I think the only good advice for him is to make sure that during the next two months or so that democracy would be given the go-ahead, because that would convey the message to the Hong Kong people that if democracy can start now, then confidence, mutual confidence can also develop. And Hong Kong, in the eyes of China, will become a totally different picture.

Now, we are all prepared to work toward that direction. The question is, how much does Mr. Xi want that to be?

Ms. BORK. Yeah. I think, regardless of what happens in the next several months, the trend is very bad. I think these arrests that came up, that Joshua Wong responded to earlier, are an extremely bad sign.

And I think also, the Congress needs to be aware of the developing sense of taboo topics and, as Mr. Lam said, the importance of being able to speak about things is vital.

Although Lord Patten talked about independence as an unrealistic objective, I think he neglected to say that the way the party treats ideas it does not like as taboos is a real problem. And regardless of whether Hong Kong people can achieve or should achieve independence, the fact that any particular political idea is not going to be allowed or will be persecuted or prosecuted, like independence, a referendum, self-determination and even democracy, is very troubling.

And if Congress can find ways, frankly, even just speaking about it, we have to begin to not allow the distortion of terms or the outlawing of terms in Hong Kong or anywhere else.

Senator COTTON. Alright, thank you all again.

Chairman RUBIO. And I have a couple of brief questions. I know the senators may need to go.

I just want to say this on the record, because I know, Mr. Lam, that eventually you are going to find your way back toward home in Hong Kong and just know we are going to continue to keep tabs on you and on your situation very carefully.

And I just want to be very clear. After your appearance here today, our view is that if any hostility comes your way upon your return, we will directly attribute that to your appearance here today and your willingness to speak truth before this commission and I believe should have a direct impact on the way we interact with the Chinese Communist Party and their government if, in fact, there is retribution sought against you for your appearance and your testimony here today.

We would take it as a deep personal affront to members of this body that you would be treated in such a way if, in fact, that is the case. We hope that it would not be the case.

We are limited on time. I promised you I would get you out of here by 11:30. I am pleased that members were able to come in the midst of everything that is going on.

I have three quick questions that I want to make sure are on the record.

And, Mr. Lee, what impact do you believe the reports under the Hong Kong Policy Act have on the situation?

Mr. LEE. I think the reports are important. And I am happy that they will be continued, because that would then give Members of Congress a clear picture as to what is happening in Hong Kong.

Now, of course, the Chinese Government will say mind your own business. But do not be deterred by that, Mr. Chairman, because you must remember that when the Sino-British Joint Declaration was first announced on the 26th of September, 1984, the U.S. Government strongly supported it, even though it was none of your business, to use the same language again.

It was a treaty between the British Government and the Chinese Government. But both governments actually worked very hard lobbying for international support. So your government was lobbied hard and gave its support. So that gives your government every justification to say, "Well, you wanted our support, we still support 'one country, two systems.' And if it is not working well because of your default, why should we not be allowed to comment on it and ask you to deliver what you already promised?"

Chairman RUBIO. Well, let me assure you, there is at least a dozen or so countries around the world that have told me to mind my own business just in the last month, and I do not.

And I would also say that the human rights of our fellow brothers and sisters around the world is our business. It should be all of our business.

And, Ms. Bork, I have read extensively the things you have written over the years on a number of issues, including this. I would just ask, and I think you touched on it briefly, but do you have any specific policy recommendations for the commission or the Congress with regard to the Hong Kong Policy Act, given the ongoing challenges to the autonomy and so forth?

I mean, we are always looking for what can we do beyond holding these hearings and I think it is very powerful, the forum of the U.S. Senate. Beyond that, what?

And if you do not, perhaps for the record later, some specific suggestions.

Ms. BORK. Certainly, but I do think the Democracy and Human Rights Act that you are working on is major in that it would completely change the outlook toward Hong Kong policy, which has been to let things move along, let China see the value of Hong Kong staying the way it is, when, frankly, I do not think a Communist party really can quite do that, certainly not without being encouraged to do so by the world's most powerful democracy.

So I would not, in any way, underestimate the importance of that addition of sanctions for misbehavior in Hong Kong. I think that is huge. And I will certainly be happy to think of some others.

I think focusing on changes in Hong Kong's law enforcement culture is really important. What is going on that they can act this way? Can you begin to focus more on the autonomy of specific institutions; the courts, the police, law enforcement, other institutions? I think that is really vital, as well.

Chairman RUBIO. And I would just say, it is a very broad question, but I think to the point you just heard Mr. Lee discuss where we are going to be told mind your own business, why is this our business? Why should, at the most basic level, why should the people who sent me here from the State of Florida support my involvement on this issue? Why does it matter to them, why does it matter to the country?

Ms. BORK. The United States has both an interest and an obligation to pursue these universal values. I mean, I think people often define them as though it is America foisting its own values. In fact, I think America, as the most powerful democracy, has the ability and the obligation to defend universal rights and freedoms for people who cannot.

There is no doubt in my mind that it benefits the United States to function in a world with more democracies, more respect for freedoms, more respect for rule of law.

And in all of my experience visiting and talking to dissidents, they welcome it. Democracy activists around the world always welcome it. They do not see it as an intrusion.

So let us think about who is saying this is interference and who is not. I really think the world's democrats struggling for their own rights and freedoms do not see it as interference at all.

Chairman RUBIO. And, Mr. Lam, I ask you, given everything that you have confronted. We hold this hearing today, it is a commission. A number of my colleagues were able to come. Others, I know, follow carefully, but because of scheduling conflicts could not.

And oftentimes, there is a feeling that what we do here is we hold these meetings and it is busywork, but it does not really make a difference because it is not a law or a program we are putting money behind.

From your perspective as someone who has been persecuted, as someone who has been harassed, as someone who has been jailed because of your advocacy for these universal principles that we all believe in or should all believe in, when we speak about these issues, when we highlight cases like yours, when we have someone like Mr. Wong here, when we talk about these issues, can you tell us what that means to someone half a world away who is confronting these challenges and is often told by the tyrants that you do not matter, no one cares about you, no one, you are on your own and you are on a losing side?

What does it mean that we do this? Is what we do here meaningful to people in your situation?

Mr. LAM. I was encouraged by more than 6,000 people going to the street to support me. So when I heard the news, I desired to come out and speak about my case.

My coming out demonstrates that all those, if we voice out the injustice, against the injustice, show that we oppose it, it will have effect and the cumulative effect will be more explicit.

If everyone who faces this oppression of China will stand up, this will have an effect to fight against such suppression. So such kinds of hearings will be definitely beneficial to a situation like mine.

Chairman RUBIO. And I agree and I thank you for being here and all of you for being here.

And I would close by telling you two examples of why this work can be rewarding. One of the cases we have discussed often in the commission, in hearings, in meetings has been the case of an American citizen, Sandy Phan-Gillis, who was unjustly jailed in China under ridiculous accusations. And we continue to raise her case, that and of her family, and that led to a positive outcome. One case among thousands that we are facing.

The other is the case in a different part of the world of Aya Hijazy who was an employee at a nongovernmental organization working on a number of very important issues on the ground in Egypt. She was jailed under ridiculous charges.

And I can tell you, when President el-Sisi of Egypt visited, there was not a meeting he had on the Hill where her case was not brought up, and that was true at his meetings in the White House, to the point where by the end of his visit he was a little annoyed. But Aya Hijazy is now in the United States along with her husband.

And one of the stories that she shared with us, that, while still imprisoned, somehow someone was able to allow them to view videos of a speech that I was able to give on the Senate floor, and others, about their cause. And it certainly emboldened them and it made them understand that they mattered.

The thing that tyrants and dictators and oppressors tell people all over the world is no one cares about you anymore, they have forgotten about you, they do not even talk about you. We are having meetings with presidents, we are cutting deals, we are doing all kinds of things, no one speaks about you. And I imagine it is designed to demoralize.

As long as the people of Florida allow me to serve here there will be at least one senator that will continue to talk about you and everyone like you in Hong Kong, in China, and all over the world. And frankly, I think there is more than just one, there are numerous of my colleagues.

And, you know, our hope is to continue to highlight human rights as a key pillar of our national security and our foreign policy. Because here is what I know, the more a country oppresses its own people, the likelier they are to create chaos and havoc and uncertainty everywhere else in the world.

Meanwhile, for the most part, free people who choose their own leaders and have economic freedom do not have time for wars. They are interested in running a business. And if their leaders go too far, they vote them out of office, because they want peace and prosperity.

Everybody has a different idea of what democracy and freedom may look like, maybe a parliamentary system, some have a house of lords, some have a senate. But the bottom line is that the greater role people have in choosing their leaders and the direction of their nations, the less likely those nations are to wage war against their neighbors and destabilize the world. And to retreat from that in this new century would not just be catastrophic, it would be tragic. And history will not be forgiving.

And so your cause is a critical component of this broader strategy. And we will continue to raise it everywhere we can. And we are just grateful that we were able to have individuals like yourselves and, in particular, you, Mr. Lam, given the risks you run being here today.

And I reiterate what I said at the outset, and I think I speak for every member of the commission and hopefully for every Member of the Senate in which I serve, that we will keep tabs and watch very closely how you are treated upon your return. We are glad you are returning. Hong Kong needs you.

And we will watch very closely. And if, in fact, retribution is taken against you, we will attribute that to your presence here today. And it will impact everything that I do and hopefully everything that the Senate does when it comes to our interaction with the Chinese Communist Party and their government.

So I thank you all for being here. I appreciate your indulgence. I apologize for the interruption, but we are grateful to you, to all of you, for your time.

And with that, the meeting of this commission is adjourned. [Applause].

Ms. MAK. And Mr. Lam would like to thank you, Mr. Chairman, and the Congress.

[Whereupon, at 11:47 a.m. the hearing was adjourned.]

APPENDIX

PREPARED STATEMENTS

PREPARED STATEMENT OF JOSHUA WONG

MAY 3, 2017

You may have known about Hong Kong's political arrangement as "One Country, Two Systems." But it has now become "One Country, One-and-a-Half Systems," and potentially "One Country, One System" in the future if conditions continue to worsen.

I was born less than a year before the handover of Hong Kong from the U.K. to China in 1997. I am 20 years old now. At the same time, the Hong Kong government is preparing its 20th handover anniversary celebration. July 1 will be the first time Xi Jinping visits Hong Kong as the Chinese President.

To pave the way for that, we now face massive political prosecution, while the government intends to disqualify democratically-elected lawmakers in the opposition camp, including the core Umbrella Movement student leader Nathan Law, who was elected last year as the youngest ever legislator at age 23. Unfortunately, Hong Kong remains far from a democracy after the Umbrella Movement.

Some people may think it is failure because we can't achieve the goal of universal suffrage but I am here to tell you today that we the spirit of the movement is in the heart of Hong Kong people. That's why I have been trying to gather more support at the international level by strengthening our collaboration around the world.

I am glad to see the reintroduction of the Hong Kong Human Rights and Democracy Act by Senators Rubio, Cotton and Cardin. Bipartisan support for the bill proves that protecting Hong Kong's freedoms and autonomy can be—and ought to be—a consensus across the political spectrum. The legislation ensures those who have participated in non-violent assembly in Hong Kong would not be denied American visas on the basis of their criminal records.

Alex Chow, who is in the audience this morning, is another core Umbrella Movement student leader. He was found guilty last July for participating in unlawful assembly, sentenced to three weeks of imprisonment with one year of suspension. Because of Alex's criminal record, he has faced significant barrier in obtaining a British student visa last year for his master's studies in London. He was recently accepted for Ph.D. studies at U.C. Berkeley this coming August, which means he will soon apply for a U.S. student visa. I cannot stress the importance of this legislation for many of those like Alex, who may potentially face difficulties entering free countries.

China's suppression against us is helped by its growing regional domination. Last year, I was invited by top Thai universities, but was not allowed to enter the country and locked up for 12 hours in a detention cell. My requests to contact a lawyer or at least notify my family in Hong Kong were both rejected. I was very worried to be the next Gui Min Hai, one of the five booksellers abducted from Thailand to China. Luckily I was finally released, but the Thai government later said that I would be forever banned to enter the country, as requested by China.

If passed, the proposed legislation will place human rights and democracy at the center of future American policy toward Hong Kong. It will send a strong signal to Beijing that as a world leader, the U.S. believes it is just as important to protect political freedom in Hong Kong as it is to protect economic freedom.

The support of the proposed legislation is also in the American interests. Hong Kong is home to around 85,000 U.S. citizens and 1,400 U.S. companies.

Two-way U.S.-Hong Kong trade was around $42 billion last year. Most American media outlets, including CNN, the Wall Street Journal, and TIME Magazine establish their Asian offices in Hong Kong.

These are all evidence that despite all the difficulties it is facing, Hong Kong remains the freest city under Chinese administration.

In conclusion, I hope democrats and republicans alike can work together to defend the fundamental human rights values they share, which Hong Kongers will continue to fight hard against Communist Regime for the day will come for us with democracy and exercise our right of self-determination.

I started my fight for democracy six years ago when I was 14. The Father of Hong Kong's Democracy, Martin Lee, is turning 79 years old this year, after four decades of struggle. I wonder, if I come to the age of 79, will I be able to see democracy?

My aspiration, and our generation's challenge is to ensure that Hong Kong continues as a beacon of human right and freedom for China and the world.

To sum up, today the authoritarian regime are dominating our future, but the day will come when we decide the future of Hong Kong. No matter what happens to the protest movement, we will reclaim the democracy that belongs to us, because time is on our side.

* * * * *

[New York Times, May 3, 2017]

STAND UP FOR DEMOCRACY IN HONG KONG

(By Joshua Wong and Jeffrey Ngo)

HONG KONG—The selection in March of the Beijing loyalist Carrie Lam as Hong Kong's next leader is the latest sign that China will continue to tighten its grip on this city. Political divisions will deepen and mistrust of the government will rise.

Ms. Lam, who was picked to be chief executive by an election committee stacked in Beijing's favor, has long taken a hard-line approach to suppressing dissent. As the former No. 2 official under the unpopular outgoing leader, Leung Chun-ying, she presided over the political reform process that ignited the Umbrella Movement of 2014, in which tens of thousands of Hong Kongers occupied major thoroughfares for three months demanding democratic rights.

With Hong Kong's autonomy plummeting to a 20-year low, it's more important than ever for Washington to affirm its commitment to freedom in Hong Kong. The Hong Kong Human Rights and Democracy Act, introduced by a bipartisan group of senators in February, would put the Hong Kong people's rights at the center of United States policy toward the semiautonomous Chinese territory.

The legislation, an update to a 1992 law governing relations between the United States and Hong Kong, would authorize the president to freeze United States-based assets of individuals who have suppressed freedoms in Hong Kong and deny them entry to America, require the secretary of state to issue an annual report on Hong Kong's political situation until at least 2023 and guarantee that Hong Kongers who have participated in nonviolent assembly would not be denied American visas on the basis of their arrest.

Our freedoms in Hong Kong have been increasingly squeezed since 2014, when the Chinese leadership in Beijing decided against democratizing the process for selecting our leader, inciting the months of protests.

A renowned legal scholar and former law school dean at Hong Kong University was denied a promotion to a top leadership post at the university because of his pro-democracy positions. Five Hong Kongers working for a bookseller that sold books critical of Beijing were abducted and taken across the border to China, where one was coerced into confessing to crimes on national television. Democratically elected lawmakers in the opposition camp have been facing costly lawsuits filed by the government to disqualify their seats. Democracy activists have been rounded up for leading protests against the government.

Beijing's fear of separatism and President Xi Jinping's uncompromising leadership style mean the situation is likely to get worse before it gets better. The Hong Kong Human Rights and Democracy Act would put much-needed pressure on American presidents to stand up to Beijing for its aggression against the people of this territory.

No United States president has visited Hong Kong since Bill Clinton in 1998. The State Department stopped issuing periodic assessments of Hong Kong's political situation in 2007. Former President Barack Obama showed only tepid support for the Hong Kong democracy movement.

President Trump hasn't spoken much yet about Hong Kong, but his China policy has been disappointing. He showed some early signs of hope when, as president-elect, he seemed willing to challenge the unjust "One China" policy on Taiwan, but he has since backed off from his tough talk against Beijing.

Congress should do its part to renew White House interest in Hong Kong, sending a message that the United States is concerned about our political freedom. Hong Kong, in spite of all the difficulties it is facing, remains the freest territory under Chinese control. For dissidents in the mainland, Hong Kong's social movements have long been sources of hope. Safeguarding what has made Hong Kong unique is in Washington's interest, especially if Americans wish to someday see a free and democratic China.

The Hong Kong Human Rights and Democracy Act—recently introduced in the Senate by Republican Senators Marco Rubio and Tom Cotton, along with Democratic Senator Benjamin Cardin—has received bipartisan backing at this early stage. American conservatives and liberals alike should support the bill and help uphold their shared values of freedom and democracy for this corner of the world.

Joshua Wong is the secretary general and a co-founder of Demosisto, a political party in Hong Kong. Jeffrey Ngo, chief researcher for Demosisto, is a master's degree student in global histories at New York University.

Follow The New York Times Opinion section on Facebook and Twitter, and sign up for the Opinion Today newsletter.

A version of this op-ed appears in print on May 4, 2017, on Page A12 of the National edition with the headline: Stand up for democracy in Hong Kong.

————

PREPARED STATEMENT OF MARTIN CHU-MING LEE

MAY 3, 2017

On the night of July 1, 1997, my home, Hong Kong, a territory of then-7 million people was handed over from Britain to the People's Republic of China. Twenty years later, we have come to a critical moment: Promised democratic development has been totally stopped, and the autonomy and core values we have worked hard to preserve under both British and Chinese rule are in serious danger.

I am 78 years old, and have been working for *four decades* as a lawyer and advocate for Hong Kong. I have been the bar chair, an elected legislator, a pro-democracy political party founder, and a member of the Basic Law drafting committee, working for the mini-Constitution agreed by China that was supposed to protect the rights of Hong Kong people.

In all of these roles, my goal has been to preserve Hong Kong's freedoms, core values, and way of life. My generation has fought hard. But it is the future generation you have heard from today, represented by Joshua Wong, whose members are even more adamant that their rights be preserved and enlarged.

The framework for the transfer of Hong Kong's sovereignty and people was established by the 1984 Joint Declaration, an international treaty registered at the United Nations. In that treaty, Hong Kong people were promised "one country, with two systems," that we could rule our affairs with a "high degree of autonomy," and that our rights, freedoms, rule of law, and way of life would continue for at least 50 years after Britain ceded Hong Kong to China

Beyond these assurances, after 150 years as a British colony, we Hong Kong people were promised that we would gradually progress toward elections based on universal suffrage. This arrangement has protected free political speech in the city and kept alive hopes for a degree of electoral democracy that we were also denied under British rule.

Twenty years ago, the "one country" part of this agreement was completed, when China assumed control over Hong Kong on July 1, 1997.

But I am here to tell you today that we are still waiting for the "two systems" promises to be upheld.

Until we are masters of our own house, you cannot say "two systems" is a reality. And without democratic elections, not one of our freedoms is secure.

Let me be clear: Hong Kong people are not challenging Beijing. We are merely asking that China uphold its pledge to let us freely choose our leaders by universal suffrage, and exercise the "high degree of autonomy" promised in the 1984 Sino-British Joint Declaration as a condition of the handover of Hong Kong.

Since the July 1, 1997 handover, Hong Kong journalists, lawyers, students, religious leaders, teachers, business executives, and other citizens have fought hard against every encroachment by Beijing. Our society is as free as it is today because of those efforts.

But much more needs to be done if Hong Kong is to remain a model for people seeking democracy and opposing authoritarianism.

We have fought to preserve our core values, including the rule of law, transparency, a free flow of information, and free markets—the values that have long been a beacon for China and beyond.

But the past three years have seen an acceleration of worrying encroachments:

 • Beijing's extrajudicial abductions of publishers and a businessman from Hong Kong;
 • The removal of elected Hong Kong leaders, by Beijing's interpretation of the Basic Law;
 • A surge in arrests of peaceful critics; and
 • Attacks on our independent judiciary.

These developments spotlight the failings of the "one country, two systems" model and the need for democratic elections to preserve basic rights and freedoms in our territory of 8 million people.

This trend also spotlights the role of the US, and the international community. The US approach in Hong Kong is governed by the US–Hong Kong Policy Act, which is rooted in the Joint Declaration, and gives the US Congress the right and obligation to speak up when freedom in Hong Kong is under threat.

Over the past four decades, Hong Kong's resilient people have weathered the announcement Hong Kong would be handed over to China, Tiananmen Square's dashing of the hope for democracy both in China and Hong Kong, and the race against time to create Hong Kong's own political institutions despite China's opposition.

This means we cherish our freedoms more, and we recognize how important their example is to any hope of a rights-respecting China in the future.

For our young people, this long road to ensuring the rights we were promised is a reminder that as Americans know from their own history, freedom is not free— it takes vigilance and persistence, a battle that sometimes extends over multiple generations.

When Hong Kong was promised by paramount leader Deng Xiaoping that we would keep all of our freedoms for 50 years after 1997 unchanged, we understood that we have to insist that every single freedom is kept intact—100%. If we do, there is a chance for those freedoms to some day come to China.

But 20 years after the handover, China's Central Liaison office in Hong Kong has gone from being a representative office to issuing pronouncements that undermine the integrity of our system.

Last week, the legal chief of the China's liaison office claimed that "one country" must come before "two systems," and suggested abrogating the treaty if Hong Kong people protest. This undermines confidence in the system, and further alienates the youth who are our future.

It is a deeply unwise statement guaranteed to generate yet more protests—obviously the opposite of what Beijing wants.

It is increasingly our young people who are literally on the frontlines of protests for democracy in Hong Kong. This includes many who weren't even born at the time of the handover in 1997.

These young people understand very well what makes Hong Kong special and different from mainland China. They have a life ahead of them based on "two systems." They don't want to live in a Hong Kong that becomes ever more like China's system of cronyism and corruption. They value academic freedom, press freedom, and the ability to protest, speak and write freely.

The young generation has now seen 20 years of the older generation trying to get Beijing to carry out its promise of two systems. They have more reason than their parents and grandparents not to trust Beijing's promises because the promises of the Basic Law have been broken.

They don't trust the present and won't wait another 20 years.

There is still a roadmap to restore relations between Hong Kong and China, which would involve Beijing discovering better judgment, as it has done before.

China needs to make sure that the "two systems" survives—both as a model for Taiwan, but also as an incentive for younger generations to stay and build on our successes.

When Xi Jinping comes to Hong Kong for the anniversary of the handover on July 1 this year, I hope he will personally reverse the dangerous course of the last two decades, and confirm that our freedoms and way of life are good for China too.

It would be helpful if the US Congress and administration reminded him that mature countries respect treaties such as the one lodged at the UN through which China pledged rights for Hong Kong if Britain agreed to give up control.

Now is the time when the world is wondering if China will be a responsible member of the global community, and the US is trying to develop a good strategic relationship with China.

Thus China needs to show the world it can be trusted to uphold international agreements and play by the rules.

What better place to start than Hong Kong—where it already obliged to do so?

PREPARED STATEMENT OF LAM WING KEE

MAY 3, 2017

MY TESTIMONY REGARDING THE "CAUSEWAY BAY BOOKS" EVENT

PROLOGUE:

Between October and December 2015, the disappearance of five persons of Causeway Bay Books in Hong Kong was investigated and confirmed by the Hong Kong media. The five were suspected to have been arrested or abducted by the Chinese government. On 17 October, GUI Minhai (shareholder) was taken away from an apartment in Pattaya, Thailand by a man. LUI Bo (shareholder) was arrested by public security people in Shenzhen while having lunch in a restaurant. CHEUNG Chiping (employee) was taken away from his home in Dongguan by armed police-men on 23 October. I myself (employee) was detained by Customs when I entered Shenzhen via the Lowu Border on 24 October, and secretly taken to Ningbo the next day. LEE Bo (shareholder) was abducted on 30 December in a warehouse carpark in Chai Wan and forcibly taken across the border to the mainland of China by nine persons.

I, LAM Wing Kee, provide my testimony below:

At 11 a.m. on 24 October 2015, I crossed the border at Lowu, Shenzhen, to meet my girlfriend in Dongguan. I was detained by Shenzhen Customs, taken onto a 7-seater car and driven to a Shenzhen police station the same day. I asked those who were taking me what crime I had committed and nobody gave any answer. Some-time after 7 o'clock in the evening, two investigative officers came to interrogate me. I had met one of them in 2012, when I was found carrying a book across the border for postal delivery to a reader. The officer taking records on that occasion was sur-named LEE, in his mid-twenties, while the person asking me questions was also surnamed LEE, in his early-fifties. On that occasion I was interrogated for over six hours and it was eventually confirmed that I really operated a bookshop in Hong Kong with no other intent.

Then the older one left the room to handle procedural matter for my release and I had a conversation with the recording officer. Because of the prior encounter, the younger Lee and I recognized each other immediately when we met again that evening. I felt a little delighted and was rather naive in thinking that China Cus-toms had mistaken me for someone else because I thought that the recording staff in his early-thirties could prove that I ran a book shop and I would be released in no time.

However, when I nodded and smiled at him, he roared at me saying that I was unrepentant even till death. I thought he was mistaken. Ever since I was held up and investigated last time, I no longer help others in bringing books across the bor-der. Through the iron bars of the custody room, I took a look of the other officer who was somewhat older. I told the one whom I recognized that I had not com-mitted wrongdoing again. Furthermore, I signed a letter of remorse last time and gave my word. Yet, upon hearing my explanation, he got even angrier. He banged on the table and rebuked: "Do you know who you are? Your sending books is in-tended at overthrowing the Chinese government. We are the Central Task Force. It is our task to impose proletariat dictatorship rule over Hong Kong people like you." I was extremely surprised, not quite believing what I heard. I know that the Central Task Force was a tool used in the Cultural Revolution to tackle class enemy and that many people were put to death by it. I sensed the seriousness of the situa-tion, but at the same time I was rather confused. To make sure, I asked him to repeat what he said. But he seemed to be aware that he had given something away. He merely stared at me, still in anger. At that time the one next to him opened a note book, signaled his colleague to sit down, and started interrogation.

The next morning, sometime past 7 am, I ate the bread given to me by the guard. I was then handcuffed, blindfolded, got a cap on my head; taken on a 7-seater car to Shenzhen train station, and changed onto a speed train. Roughly 13–14 hours later, we arrived at Ningbo Station. Throughout the journey I was anxious and rest-less, eager to know where I was being taken. Though I was tied to the iron seat and despite the fact that I had not slept the night before, I tried hard to keep up spirit and paid attention to the stops made. When we got off the train, I peeked through the fringe of the eye mask and saw an illuminated station sign: Ningbo sta-tion. The car used after we got off the train was probably also a 7-seater. I was placed in the middle seat at the back with people by my two sides. After 40 minutes or so, I was held to go up to the 1st floor of a building and then into a room. When the handcuffs, eye mask and cap were taken away, sudden exposure to light pre-vented them from opening fully. Before I could see the environment clearly, I was told to go to a corner where there was a half-translucent screen, six-and-a-half ft. high and serving as partition for a squat-type latrine. I was told to take off all my clothes, squatted and stretched out my arms and feet for examination. Then I changed into prisoner top, orange in colour, and cotton sweat pants in cement-like colour. What crime have I committed? As my glasses were taken from me when I boarded the train blindfolded, I was directing my question at people with blurred faces. Again I got no reply.

I was waken up at 7:30 in the morning. I washed and brushed up; and later had breakfast at 8 a.m. It included congee of corn which had been grinded like sesame, a bun, fried egg and pickle etc. As I was about to eat, the guard standing by the screen came close for fear that I might take some other action. As I ate, I made observation of the surrounding. The previous night I was so tired that when they pointed a bed to me indicating I could lie down, I tumbled into it and readily fell asleep. Once I finished eating, the guard immediately removed the plastic meal box and plastic spoon and handed them to another guard at the door. The one sitting at the door kept staring at me with his arms crossed. I knew that there would be interrogation later, so I made use of the time gap to think things over and figure out the situation. From where I was merely a day ago, I was taken to this place a thousand miles away. I picked up one of the plastic slippers they gave me and inspected the sole. It bore the place of manufacture: Ningbo. Is this place Ningbo? I showed the slipper to the guards. Both of them were still young and had an air of innocence, apparently not yet nurtured into "angry youths." Although I repeatedly asked many times what crime I had committed, no answer was given still. I turned my head and saw that the other guard behind was also staring at me. At that moment two persons entered.

One was a tall big guy who did not identify himself. He later said that he surnamed SHI. He was the chief interrogator. The other one, who had about the same height as mine, should be the assistant. They started by asking my name, address in Hong Kong, job, position and why ownership of the bookshop was transferred to Mighty Current etc., which were about the same questions asked during the interrogation in Shenzhen. Then I was asked about the mailing of books: when did it start, the kind of books sent, how many had been sent, the means of sending etc. I gave factual answers while SHI, who remained expressionless on his face throughout, made record on computer. At that point I made further attempt to ask: what crime had I committed? The tall guy kept on typing without any response. I looked at the other one. Leaning against the back of chair, he looked at me with a strange expression in his eyes, surprised that I was unaware of a serious disaster to come. Mr. SHI gave me a piece of paper and told me to sign. It included two statements: one was to voluntarily give up the right to notify my family, another was to voluntarily give up the right to employ a lawyer.

Interrogation continued like that, from 4 or 5 times a week in November to 2 or 3 times a week in December. They brought up questions about co-workers in the bookshop: GUI Minhai, LEE Bo, CHEUNG Chiping and how I got to know them. I answered factually to the best of my knowledge. At that time, I had no idea of their lock-up yet. GUI Minhai, in particular, was abducted in Thailand on 17 October 2015. LEE Bo disappeared in the evening of 30 December 2015, whereas LUI Bo and CHEUNG Chiping had their mishap even earlier than me: LUI Bo on 14 October 2015 in Shenzhen and CHEUNG Chiping on 23 October in Dongguan. (CHEUNG Chiping himself told me about the date of his mishap when the four of us met over dinner in "Unicorn Hill" in Shenzhen, under the arrangement of the Chinese investigative staff handling our cases. It was in the same evening that I was told by LUI Bo that his arrest took place in a restaurant in Shenzhen.) In mid-December 2015, the guy surnamed SHI showed me some computer records which startled me. Those were records of postal purchases with the book shop from September 2013 to October 2015. Names, telephone numbers and addresses of all subscribers, overseas and in mainland China, and even the number of books ordered and postal record numbers were there. Everything was shown clearly. As I viewed the screen, I quietly wondered how they managed to get the information of readers' book orders. Did they get hold of my key and sent people to the book shop to steal? Could they be so audacious and reckless as to engage in cross-border jurisdiction?

Indeed they were audacious and reckless enough to carry out cross-border jurisdiction. In an interview with "Initium Media" in Hong Kong before his disappearance, LEE Bo had clearly indicated that he would not enter mainland China. The interview was conducted in November 2015. Yet he suddenly disappeared on 30 December. Two days later, his wife found his Home Return Permit in a drawer. LEE Bo returned to Hong Kong in March 2016 to cancel the case which had been reported to the police. He met the media and said that he smuggled into China so as to assist the mainland authority in some investigation. He was clearly not telling the truth It was merely because his child was in Fujian that he was compelled to cooperate. Furthermore, when I went to LEE Bo's office on 14 and 15 June 2016 to get hold of the computer (with records of postal-order subscribers) at the request of SHI, LEE privately told me twice that he had been taken away and escorted to the mainland by some people. Although he denied this afterwards, it is really not difficult to infer from various details of the case that LEE Bo was forced to go to the mainland against his wish. Obviously, the Chinese government has inflicted damage to the One-country, two-systems and violated its assurance to Hong Kong people under the Basic Law.

I was alone and helpless. I am not sure if it was the endless interrogation or infinite custody without charge that made me start to consider suicide in just 3 months. Whenever I looked carefully, I could see that the four walls were covered with soft pads. Obviously, any attempt to break my neck by knocking against the wall would not work. The ceiling was close to 20 ft. high, and there was no way I could twist my pants into rope for hanging on it. There was a big inaccessible window, with iron bars blocked by barbed wire which could not be opened with bare hands. The shower head, installed high up, was arc-shaped and could not hang anything. The more one looked at the set-up of the room, the more one got frightened because, clearly, long-term solitary confinement and isolation must have resulted in nervous breakdown for somebody and led to suicide in the past. All the measures in the room were aimed at preventing suicide. I was probably in such a state of mind when the idea of suicide came up. I think I did not feel too frightened of death itself because, after all, every person must die. It is the fear of death that I feared. All of a sudden, I seemed to be experiencing the inner feelings of someone with desire to die.

Around the middle of January 2016, they brought a document for me to read. It was a letter of confession regarding a charge against me: "Selling books illegally." The letter head was The People's Republic of China. The date—in year, month and day—was given at the bottom. I held my head up. The assistant staff wanted me to sign, similar to the day when I was imprisoned in Ningbo and asked to sign those statements of giving-up my rights. I thought that since I had signed on the previous occasion, there was no way not to sign this time although I knew that such method in handling the case was illegal. Fine. Upon signing, Mr Shi had a more relaxed expression on his face. Then he turned on the computer and asked me to identify some people. I leaned forward to view the screen. It was information relating to postal delivery for readers. Some readers placed orders via email. I never met them. Some people came to the shop to make purchases for postal delivery. "Who is this person, do you know?" I saw the names against the cursor. They were ordinary readers, I told him. I did not know their background. Then a few more were pointed out to me to see if I were familiar with them. I kept shaking my head. They knew I would cooperate.

Several days later, I was asked to write a letter of remorse. Actually I had not committed any crime. I did not know how to write such a letter. Somehow I began like this: "Because I have committed a crime, I now sincerely express regret to the Chinese government . . ." With difficulty I waffled on and managed to fill up an A4 sheet. The next day the assistant staff came to take the sheet away, probably to be handed to SHI for inspection. I thought my half-hearted confession would work. I went to the window and viewed up the sky again. The opposite building was visible from this side. Sometimes I gave the excuse of using the toilet and tip-toed on the raised step of the squatting toilet to look outside. I counted 20 big windows on the opposite building. It had 5-stories, probably the same for the building where I was. There were a few more buildings on the right. If there was no mist, I could see the top of several hills. Later, when there was arrangement to make video recording of me, I was moved to another room along the corridor. There, I could see that next to another building at the back was also a small hill. I reckoned that I was detained in a place surrounded by hills on three sides. Misty in the morning and at night, it should be a basin. Furthermore, when I was taken outside during that period, blindfolded, and driven by car to another place for taking my confession video, both exit and return entry were made through the right-hand side at the back, which means there must have been only one entrance. Therefore I was even more certain about it. Later on, news reports in Hong Kong said that we were kept in custody in Ci Xi Detention Centre of Ningbo. That was probably a mistake. As seen from photos of the Ci Xi Detention Centre, the place does not appear to be a basin. Besides, I had subtly taken a peep at the entrance which was only an electric gate with no sign whatsoever.

Around January to February, I signed the letters of confession and remorse. I thought the case would soon be over. With all procedures completed, one only has to wait for sentencing by the Court. SHI provided a case for my reference. In 2011, a person from north-eastern China had also committed the crime of "Selling books illegally," involving a sum of over three hundred thousand dollars. In the end he was given a jail term of five years. SHI said that if the Chinese government held me responsible for the criminal guilt since the change in ownership of the book shop, and because the sum involved in mail delivery of books was not high, somewhat over a hundred thousand dollars only, most likely the sentence would be two years. At that time I had already given in to fate. I know that the Court is merely for show. The so-called courts in China are only responsible for passing sentences, as all suspects are already regarded as convicts once the trial procedure is completed. Solicitors are employed merely for the purpose of making pleads. Little did I know the situation was more complicated than that. They later showed me some books, about eight or nine of them, all being publications of Mighty Current. SHI picked a few and asked me about the contents, source of information and whether I knew the authors. I explained to him that I was only engaged in the selling of books and was not knowledgeable about the things he asked because those were publication matters. Only the bosses GUI Minhai and LEE Bo knew all about the publications of Mighty Current. Not long afterwards, I was told I could get a bail but before that, I had yet to wait for people from Beijing to examine my behavior.

By then confession videos had already been taken. The recording process took place six or seven times in the room where I was imprisoned, and three times in another place where they took me there in a 7-seater car. After leaving the building, the drive took about 45 minutes, passing through an express highway and ending up in a big complex with many low-rise houses. All the recording of so-called confession was conducted in accordance with the script they gave me which I followed. Mr. SHI doubled as the director. The weirdest incident happened on one occasion when I was taken to a building. After getting off the car in the carpark, there was a staircase. Probably to save trouble, they removed my eye mask to let me walk the stairs myself. After getting down to the lowest floor and along the passage way, a policewoman walked past by, facing me directly. On her shoulder was the badge of Ningbo Public Security Bureau. Same as on the previous occasion, I got into the same room and took the prisoner seat. While preparation was being made for recording, the policewoman came in too, having changed into civilian clothing, and sat by the wall. "Miss Fong? "asked Mr. SHI, who was seated in an interrogator's stand like that in court. The policewoman nodded. He opened the document on the desk and briefly examined it. Then he said it was fine for Miss Fong to remain seated. She nodded. Camera was turned on by the assistant at the back and with the two sitting side by side, questions and answers progressed in sequence, following prior rehearsal. When recording was finished, I asked SHI out of curiosity, "What was the seated lady doing there?" He removed the recording equipment and answered me at the same time, "She is a witness." I could not withhold my surprise. She was undoubtedly a policewoman, with no connection to my case whatsoever. They found themselves a so-called witness just like that? It was utterly unbelievable how reckless they were, not to mention that the case had been handled in an unlawful manner all along.

I could not help worrying because of what happened afterwards. For the purpose of making application for bail, a remorse video had been made. It was submitted to Beijing along with the letter of remorse. While waiting for news about the outcome, one day I heard SHI said that the higher authority was not satisfied. What was to be done? I was terribly anxious. If no approval forthcoming, I would be in jail for the Chinese New Year. Several days later, further news was heard. Beijing would send people here. To observe me, it was said. Right away I felt that it was ominous. One afternoon, two persons came in. I was squatting by the toilet and washing clothes. I hurriedly returned to my seat. I waited till they were seated. I was about to sit down when one of them suddenly banged the table and said I was not allowed to sit. I was startled, and had to remain standing. The other person started to talk, "Do you know who we are?" I shook my head, still in shock. Then the other person banged the table also. "We belong to the Central Task Force from Beijing. The kind of books you publish defame our national leaders. People like you are vicious to the extreme, not worthy of pardon. We can impose proletariat dictatorship over you for ten, twenty years, even till death. No one in Hong Kong knows. We can even pinch you to death like a bug." I was dumbfounded by such sudden abusive outbursts and did not know what to do. I could only stare blankly, incapable of any reaction but to let them continue their rounds of relentless cursing. I had no idea how long the outbursts lasted. I kept standing there. Not until two guards entered later did I realize that they had left. Very clearly, release on bail was out of the question.

Let's make another videos; write another letter of remorse, said SHI later. So the video was re-made, and a letter of remorse written again for submission. By then the Chinese New Year was drawing near. SHI knew I was so worried that I suffered from insomnia. Maybe he wanted to help. He showed friendly gesture. I am not sure if it was due to similarity in our sentiments or interests, or whether there was some other reason. I understood that he was following orders to interrogate me. He was a little sympathetic towards me, hoping that I could get released on bail. Later, he even said to me that he would be ready to write a letter of plead and be my guarantor, as long as I cooperate in the future. At that time I had no choice but to believe him.

Strangely, SHI came several days later to say that approval from the higher authority had come; our fates were tied together; that he would be ruined by me if I jumped bail. I felt relieved and my heart was at ease. I certainly felt grateful for Mr SHI's assistance from the bottom of my heart and promised that I would definitely cooperate with him in the future. However, as I recall the matter now, things looked somewhat suspicious. Based on my observation of Mr SHI, I still believe in him. He was only used as a pawn in a situation that bundled him and me together. That had been deliberately arranged by others, it seems.

I am not groundless in saying the above. Why did Beijing suddenly send people to berate me like mad? While release bail seemed very remote, somebody knew that Mr SHI would righteously give a hand. That somebody could well be his boss. He understood Mr SHI. And Mr SHI was both a police officer and an educated person. Educated people have their own mentality and at the same time sympathy for others. They tend to be more sympathetic than ordinary folks. If Mr SHI and I were somehow bundled together on the same boat, the risk of me jumping bail would be reduced, because I could not flee on my own and forsake someone who had helped me. The situation was even more obvious if my case was compared with the three others who had been taken to the mainland. They all had relatives in the mainland whereas I only had a girlfriend there. That was how I viewed Mr SHI then. Apart from that, facts which I observed later on indicate that the whole affair involved some scheme even more horrid.

One afternoon SHI came over and said that a half-length photo was to be taken. The person who came along was not the assistant but the person surnamed LEE whom I previously knew in Shenzhen. When I got up, he held the camera with one hand and pushed me towards the wall with the other. He told me to keep a good standing posture, and held up the camera to take photos. Every time a photo was taken, the camera flashed. I blinked my eyes at the flare, and he examined the image. It did not seem to work because every time a photo was taken, I blinked and my eyes were closed in all the photos. Seeing that LEE could not manage, Mr SHI took over the camera, made some adjustment and turned off the flash. He took several photos consecutively, examined them and nodded to indicate the job was done. I returned to my seat. Mr SHI went to the door, looked back over his shoulder and told me I could leave in a few days but would have to stay for a while in Shaoguan first. As I saw him disappear, I realized that he too also belonged to the Central Task Force.

I could not leave China when I was I on bail. After the Chinese New Year i.e. in end-March 2016, they placed me in Shaoguan. I worked in a library for free until June. Then arrangement was made for me to return to Hong Kong to report to the police to cancel my case. I would visit my family and bring back the computer hard disk storing records of subscribers. I asked them why was the hard disk required when they already had all the software information. SHI said it was because the books were posted by me and the data had been input by me. Therefore I would have to bring it back to serve as evidence in court, to make prosecution against those subscribers more forceful. Such a request by SHI obviously meant that they wanted me to betray other people. At that time I had no choice but to agree involuntarily. On 14 June 2016, I took express rail to Shenzhen under the surveillance of accompanying people. Besides SHI, the other one was Supervisor CHAN. They asked me to cross the border first because they didn't want to be seen crossing border with me, lest exposing themselves in conducting cross-border surveillance. Later on, when I made statement at the police station in Wanchai and viewed the recorded video, I could see that I crossed the Lowu Bridge at 11:25 whereas they could be seen at 11:55. At 12:15:30, they appeared at the exit of immigration.

After careful thought, I met the press on 16 June 2016 accompanied by Mr. Albert HO Chun-yan of the Democratic Party of Hong Kong. The event was made public. All to be said has been said, but I have one thing to add. In the middle of November 2015, the Central Task Force asked a local gangster surnamed CHAN, to acquire ownership of Causeway Bay Books from Lee Bo, pre-paid the rental for two years with over HK$ 1 million, with the intention that I would resume work there. (Mr. SHI said to me in Shaoguan that arrangement would be made for me to return to the book shop and that I would have to remain in touch with him.) Hong Kong people or people from the mainland of China making purchases in the book shop would be monitored. In other words, the book shop would be a point of surveillance. Undoubtedly, the whole affair shows that the Chinese government tries to restrain the freedom of speech and freedom of publication in Hong Kong. Such illegal activity has been carried out with elaborate planning and careful arrangement throughout.

LAM Wing Kee

Manager of Causeway Bay Books (ex-owner of the book shop)
10 April 2017

PREPARED STATEMENT OF ELLEN BORK

MAY 3, 2017

Mr. Chairman and members of the Commission, it is an honor to appear before you alongside leaders of Hong Kong's democracy movement. Thank you for including me in today's hearing.

As we approach the 20th anniversary of Hong Kong's return to mainland Chinese rule, a great deal has changed.

Beijing has dropped the pretense of respect for Hong Kong's autonomy and the "one country, two systems" arrangement. The Party is not only preventing Hong Kong from moving forward toward full democracy, it is also advancing communist political culture and taboos within Hong Kong's society. Even words like "referendum" and "self-determination" are being treated as taboo.

Hong Kong's democracy movement has responded in ways that few expected. Beijing's refusal to allow democratic election of the chief executive sparked the Umbrella movement protests of 2014. The movement's young leaders have eclipsed the established leadership that started the movement in the 1980s. The old guard is thrilled. They have happily given way to the new generation, many of whom were infants, or not yet born when the movement accelerated after the 1989 Tiananmen crackdown.

Unlike their parents and grandparents, young Hong Kong democrats don't have firsthand experience of living under mainland communist rule. They see no reason for their futures to be constrained by arrangements reached by Great Britain and China without input or assent of the Hong Kong people—particularly now that the UK seeks to be Beijing's "best partner in the West." They raise an issue that has been largely overlooked by the U.S. and the world's other democracies: even the inadequate guarantees of the Joint Declaration will expire in 2047.

Hong Kong people's identity has changed—or been revealed—under communist rule. Fewer identify as Chinese or as citizens of the PRC. Their outlook is shaped by their experience living in Hong Kong's free society, as well as their expectation that they would be allowed preserve it, and establish full democracy.

U.S. policy has not changed in response to these developments. Adopted in 1992, before the handover, the U.S.-Hong Kong Policy Act was a product of optimism about Hong Kong's future and a belief that Beijing would tolerate "two systems" within its borders. The approach to Hong Kong was part and parcel of the "engagement" approach toward China. At the time, the US was enjoying victory in the Cold War with the Soviet Union. American policymakers were taken by Francis Fukuyama's famous essay, The End of History. The triumph of democracy over communism, fascism, marked " the end point of mankind's ideological evolution and the universalization of Western liberal democracy as the final form of human government." Confrontation could be avoided. Trade and investment, and integration into the world system would change China.

It wasn't a big jump from that idea to a belief that that China's Communist Party would accept Hong Kong's rule of law, capitalism, and civil liberties. The hope was expressed that Hong Kong would change China, not the other way around. At the very least, people argued, Beijing would want to keep Hong Kong as it was for economic reasons. The Party would not, the argument went, want to "kill the goose that laid the golden egg."

If Beijing did interfere in Hong Kong, lawmakers contemplated that the president could downgrade Hong Kong's separate status in some areas of U.S. law. However, the executive has been understandably reluctant to take that step. Denying Hong Kong separate treatment would penalize the people of Hong Kong, not Beijing's Party leaders or even their proxies in Hong Kong. The act's approach toward Hong Kong has lasted well after conditions for which it was adopted changed.

New legislation proposed by members of the commission, the Hong Kong Human Rights and Democracy Act, would take an important step by shifting the consequences for the most egregious violations of Hong Kong's autonomy from the people of Hong Kong to those who are actually responsible.

Members should consider broadening this provision. China's seizures of the booksellers are not isolated incidents. Beijing has also reached across borders to pursue Tibetans in Nepal and Uighurs in Central and Southeast Asia. It has coerced Thailand to repatriate Chinese dissidents. When the United Kingdom's Foreign Secretary sought to intercede on behalf of Lee Bo, a British citizen and one of the Hong Kong booksellers, the Chinese foreign minister rebuffed him, saying Lee is "first and foremost a Chinese citizen." This is an alarming distortion of norms of sovereignty and citizenship, but one that so far seems to have elicited little response from the countries involved or from Washington. Although Great Britain declared a "serious breach" of the Joint Declaration in connection with the booksellers, it's not clear what that means since London has gone on to conduct business as usual with China.

For a long time, the U.S. has treated Hong Kong as a discrete issue. We hoped that Party leaders would tolerate freedoms there that they would not allow in the mainland. On America's behalf, Secretary of State Albright insisted that there would be U.S.-China relations would suffer if Beijing didn't live up to its promises under the Joint Declaration. However, we effectively, and probably deliberately sidelined ourselves by taking the position that the U.S. could not express an opinion on violations of a treaty to which it was not a party.

It is clear now, even more than it was in 1997, that America has the leading role in support for Hong Kong's democracy, rule of law and civil liberties. Hong Kong's fate will be determined not by arguments over a treaty signed by a disinterested, fading colonial power, but by the confidence and commitment to democratic norms and institutions by the U.S. and its allies.

From support for the Helsinki movement in the Soviet bloc, to the defense of Taiwan, to the battles over MFN for China, Congress has long played an indispensible role in making democracy and human rights a priority in America's foreign policy. Considering the Trump administration's affinity for autocrats, Congress's responsibility to maintain principled support for democracy around the world is even greater now and in the years ahead.

————

PREPARED STATEMENT OF HON. MARCO RUBIO, A U.S. SENATOR FROM FLORIDA; CHAIRMAN, CONGRESSIONAL-EXECUTIVE COMMISSION ON CHINA

MAY 3, 2017

Good morning. This is a hearing of the Congressional-Executive Commission on China. The title of this hearing is "Will the Hong Kong Model Survive?: An Assessment 20 Years After the Handover."

We will have two panels testifying today. The first panel will feature the Right Honourable Lord Patten of Barnes—Christopher Patten—testifying via video link from London. Lord Patten, in addition to serving in the House of Lords was the last British Governor of Hong Kong, and oversaw the transfer to China twenty years ago this July.

The second panel will include:

- Joshua Wong, "Umbrella Movement" Leader and Secretary-General of the new Hong Kong political party, Demosistō;
- Martin Lee, Barrister, founding Chairman of the Democratic Party of Hong Kong, former Member of the Drafting Committee for the Basic Law, and former Member of the Legislative Council of Hong Kong (1985–2008);
- Lam Wing Kee, Founder, Causeway Bay Books, one of five forcibly disappeared Hong Kong booksellers; and
- Ellen Bork, a writer whose work on democracy and human rights as a priority in American foreign policy has appeared in the Wall Street Journal, the Washington Post and the Financial Times among other publications.
- I would also note that translating for Mr. Lam is Ms. Mak Yin Ting, a journalist and veteran leader of the Hong Kong Journalists Association, the territory's leading defender of press freedom.

Thank you all for being here. As has already been noted, today's hearing is timely given the 20th anniversary, this July, of the British handover of Hong Kong. Rewatching film footage and commentary of that historic day, we can't help but take note of the pageantry: the raising and lowering of flags, solemn handshakes and national anthems.

Many observers described the handover as signifying the sunset of a once great colonial power and the ascent of a rising China. But there was and remains far more at stake.

On that day in 1997 Lord Patten—who we'll hear from momentarily—spoke of Hong Kong's "unshakable destiny"—a Hong Kong governed by and for the people of Hong Kong. And it is that destiny that animates today's gathering.

However, in recent years, Beijing has consistently undermined the 'one country, two systems' principle and infringed on the democratic freedoms that the residents of Hong Kong are supposed to be guaranteed under the Sino-British Joint Declaration—an international treaty—and Hong Kong's Basic Law.

The rise of "localist" politicians and activists who call for greater political and legal self-determination for Hong Kong has drawn harsh reprisals from the Chinese and Hong Kong governments.

The Chinese government's November 2016 interpretation of Hong Kong's Basic Law effectively prohibited two recently elected Hong Kong legislators from taking office and was viewed as a blow to Hong Kong's judicial independence. The Hong Kong government is currently seeking the removal from office of four other pro-democratic legislators along the same lines.

In March of this year, nine activists were arrested for their participation in the Occupy Central protests in 2014, including two sitting pro-democratic lawmakers.

Their arrests came less than 24 hours after the undemocratic "election" of Carrie Lam to serve as Hong Kong's next Chief Executive, drawing widespread condemnation and accusations of a retaliatory campaign aimed at punishing leaders of the Hong Kong democracy movement and suppressing dissent prior to her taking office.

In late 2015, five Hong Kong-based booksellers, including one of today's witnesses, were disappeared or abducted to mainland China. One of these booksellers, Gui Minhai, a Swedish citizen abducted from Thailand, remains in custody in China, where he will mark his 53rd birthday this Friday.

The disappearances and abductions of the booksellers, and their coerced "confessions" which were broadcast on Hong Kong television, sent shockwaves through the city and are reflective of a larger troubling trend in the area of press freedom and freedom of expression.

Today is World Press Freedom Day and it bears mentioning that the recently released Reporters Without Borders index ranking countries for their press freedom environment had Hong Kong slipping 4 places in a single year.

In February, Senators Cardin and Cotton joined me in introducing the bipartisan *Hong Kong Human Rights and Democracy Act,* which would renew the United States' historical commitment to Hong Kong at a time when its autonomy is increasingly under assault.

The legislation also establishes punitive measures against government officials in Hong Kong or mainland China who are responsible for suppressing basic freedoms in Hong Kong.

Looking ahead, Congress will be closely watching how Hong Kong authorities and the mainland handle the 20th anniversary as well as whether Ms. Lam moves to reintroduce Article 23, widely despised anti-subversion and anti-sedition legislation first proposed in 2002, which triggered massive protests in which half a million Hong Kongers took to the streets.

I look forward to today's hearing. Without question, there are many layers and complexities to our relationship with China as evidenced by the questions during yesterday's hearing for Governor Branstad to serve as U.S. ambassador to China.

Despite the multitude of challenges, Hong Kong's future, indeed its destiny, must not be sidelined. China's assault on democratic institutions and human rights is of central importance to the people of Hong Kong and to its status as a free market, economic powerhouse and hub for international trade and investment.

We cannot allow Hong Kong to go the way of Beijing's failed authoritarianism and one-party rule.

PREPARED STATEMENT OF HON. CHRISTOPHER H. SMITH, A U.S. REPRESENTATIVE FROM NEW JERSEY; COCHAIRMAN, CONGRESSIONAL-EXECUTIVE COMMISSION ON CHINA

MAY 3, 2017

Two and half years ago, tens of thousands of Hong Kong's residents peacefully gathered in the streets, yellow umbrellas in hand, seeking electoral reform and greater democracy. Joshua Wong was at the forefront of that movement—along with Nathan Law and Alex Chow and so many young student leaders. The Umbrella Movement was not only composed of students, but included veterans of the democracy movement in Hong Kong, including Martin Lee.

It is good to see Joshua and Martin here today, bringing together the generations of advocates committed to Hong Kong's freedom and autonomy.

Joshua Wong and all those associated with the Umbrella Movement have become important symbols of Hong Kong's vitality and its freedoms. They are now part of Hong Kong's unique brand and any effort to detain, censor, or intimidate them damages that brand.

Over the past two years, Senator Rubio and I, along with other members of the China Commission, have introduced the Hong Kong Human Rights and Democracy Act and we have worked in Congress to maintain the State Department's annual report on Hong Kong.

We have issued statements of concern about the political prosecutions of Joshua and other Umbrella Movement leaders; the unprecedented interventions by the Chinese government in Hong Kong's courts and political affairs, and the abductions Hong Kong booksellers and other citizens.

We have also discussed the erosion of Hong Kong's autonomy and freedoms with both U.S. and Chinese officials.

I want to commend Senator Rubio for his leadership on human rights issues and on Hong Kong. We have worked together closely and I am honored to work with him on the China Commission. Senator Rubio is a true champion of the globe's oppressed and persecuted.

As long as I have the privilege of serving as a Chair of the China Commission, I promise to continue shining a light on Hong Kong. Maintaining Hong Kong's autonomy is a critical U.S. interest.

The U.S. also has a clear interest in Beijing abiding by its international agreements—in Hong Kong and elsewhere.

The democratic aspirations of the people of Hong Kong cannot be indefinitely suppressed. I promise to stand with Hong Kong and call attention to violations of basic human rights as long as I serve in Congress.

Though Beijing's increasingly rough oversight of Hong Kong may not be as brutal as that pursued on the Mainland, it is no less pernicious. The ultimate goal is eroding Hong Kong's guaranteed freedoms and the rule law and intimidating those who try to defend them.

This year will be the 20th anniversary of the handover of Hong Kong. Unfortunately it seems the territory's autonomy looks increasingly fragile.

We are coming up on another anniversary as well, the 25th anniversary of the Hong Kong Policy Act.

At this juncture we should be examining both the health of the "one country, two systems" model and examining the very assumptions that underlie U.S.-Hong Kong relations. What can be done differently, what new priorities should be set?

The Hong Kong Policy Act of 1992 was based on the assumption that freedom, the rule of law, and autonomy promised to Hong Kong would be protected and respected.

It was also based on the assumption that time was on the side of freedom—that trade and investment would eventually bring political liberalization and human rights to Mainland China.

As Chairman Rubio and I have been saying for some time, one can no longer base U.S. policy on the "fantasy" that China's future will be more democratic and more open.

Mainland China has become more repressive, not less. Prosperity has turned a poor authoritarian country into a rich authoritarian country with predictable results for China's rights defenders, ethnic and religious groups, labor and democracy advocates, foreign businesses and Hong Kong's autonomy.

Some will argue that the best course of action would be to retreat into a hard realism, recognize China's interests and spheres of influence and protect U.S. interests. We could ignore what is happening in Hong Kong and shift responsibility to the British or some undefined international body.

I disagree.

We don't need a new realism to govern our China policy. Instead, we need a new idealism—a renewed commitment to democratic ideals, to human rights, and the rule of law in ways that compete directly with the Chinese model in Asia and Africa and elsewhere.

Chinese leaders need to know that the United States stands for freedom of expression, the freedom of religion, Internet freedom, the rule of law, universal suffrage, and an end to torture as critical interests, necessary for bilateral relations, and linked to the expansion of mutual prosperity and integrated security.

The U.S. should also push back hard against the erosion of freedom and autonomy in Hong Kong.

It is in everyone's interest that Hong Kong remain a free and prosperous bridge between China and the West, but the city's unique vitality and prosperity are rooted in its guaranteed freedoms. If Hong Kong is to become just another Mainland Chinese city, we will have to reassess whether Hong Kong warrants special status under U.S. law.

The arc of history does not bend toward justice without concerted action from all freedom-loving peoples. If the U.S. and the international community does not defend the rights and freedoms of Hong Kong's citizens now, there is little hope that freedom can take root in China's future.

SUBMISSION FOR THE RECORD

WILL THE HONG KONG MODEL SURVIVE? AN ASSESSMENT 20 YEARS AFTER THE HANDOVER

MAY 3, 2017

Witness Biographies

The Rt. Hon. the Lord Patten of Barnes CH, 28th Governor of Hong Kong, 1992–1997

Lord Patten of Barnes (Christopher) was a Conservative Member of Parliament from 1979 to 1992, was a Minister in the Governments of both Margaret Thatcher and John Major, and was Chairman of the Conservative Party from 1990 to 1992. From 1992 to 1997 he was the last British Governor of Hong Kong. In 1998 and 1999 he chaired the independent Commission on Policing in Northern Ireland and from 1999 to 2004 was the European Commissioner for External Affairs. He helped to organize Pope Benedict's visit to the United Kingdom in 2010 and became Chairman of the Vatican Media Advisory Committee for Pope Francis in 2014. From 2011 to 2014 he was Chairman of the BBC Trust. He was elected Chancellor of Oxford University in 2003—a post he still holds. He is the author of several books including "East and West" on his experiences as Governor of Hong Kong; "Not Quite the Diplomat" on his experience as a European Commissioner; and "What Next—Surviving the 21st Century"—a book on international politics.

Martin Lee, Barrister, founding Chairman of the Democratic Party of Hong Kong, former Member of the Drafting Committee for the Basic Law, and former Member of the Legislative Council of Hong Kong (1985–2008)

Martin C.M. Lee is a veteran political leader and rule of law advocate in Hong Kong. He is the founding chairman of the territory's first political party, the Democratic Party (1994–2002), one of the largest and most popular political parties in Hong Kong. Mr. Lee is a Senior Counsel (formerly Queen's Counsel). He has been chair of Hong Kong's Bar Association, and was an elected member of the Legislative Council from 1985 to 2008. Mr. Lee has been a champion of democracy in Hong Kong for four decades, insisting that the territory's freedoms, human rights, and the rule of law must be underpinned by democratic institutions if the territory is to continue to prosper as part of China. He has not been allowed to visit Mainland China since the Tiananmen Massacre on 4 June 1989. The European People's Party and European Democrats in the European Parliament named Mr. Lee the first non-European recipient of the Schuman Medal in 2000. In 1997, the National Endowment for Democracy presented Mr. Lee its annual Democracy leadership Award. In 1996, Liberal International awarded Mr. Lee the Prize for Freedom.

Joshua Wong, "Umbrella Movement" Leader and Secretary-General, Demosistō

Joshua Wong is the secretary-general of Demosistō, a new political party he co-founded in Hong Kong. He came to world attention as the 14-year old convener of the student group Scholarism, a student-led movement opposing the Chinese government's efforts to interfere in school curriculums through the government's planned "patriotic education" policy. Against long odds, Scholarism succeeded in getting the government to withdraw its pernicious plan, a story shown in the new award-winning documentary film, "Joshua: Teenager vs Superpower." Joshua Wong joined other youth and civic leaders in Hong Kong as a core student organizer of the 2014 Umbrella Movement, pressing the government to honor longstanding promises of democratic elections. Joshua Wong was nominated for TIME's 2014 Person of the Year, named one of the 25 Most Influential Teens by TIME, one of the World's 50 Greatest Leaders by Fortune, and one of the 100 Leading Global Thinkers by Foreign Policy.

Lam Wing Kee, Founder, Causeway Bay Books, one of five forcibly disappeared Hong Kong booksellers

Lam Wing Kee is one of five booksellers who were forcibly disappeared in 2015 and later paraded on Chinese television. Mr. Lam founded Causeway Bay Books in 1994 and sold it to Mighty Current publishing house in 2014. On October 24, 2015, he entered China and was detained. After almost eight months, on June 14, 2016, he was released back to Hong Kong with instructions to contact Hong Kong police to drop his missing person case, retrieve evidence for Chinese authorities, and return to China to be under residential surveillance. Instead, on June 16, he decided to go public about his ordeal.

Ellen Bork, writer

Ellen Bork writes frequently about democracy and human rights as a priority in American foreign policy. She worked for the U.S. Department of State in the mid-1980s. In the late 1990s, she served on Capitol Hill as a legislative assistant to Senator Connie Mack and as the senior professional staff member for East Asia and the Pacific on the Senate Foreign Relations Committee under Chairman Jesse Helms. She has worked most recently at the Foreign Policy Initiative and at Freedom House. She is writing a book about America's strategic interest in Tibet. She contributed the article "The Rise of Taiwan," about Taiwan's democratic civic identity and the challenge it poses to the "one China" policy, to "The Rise of China" (Gary Schmitt editor, Encounter Books, 2009). Her articles have been published the Wall Street Journal, the Washington Post, the Financial Times, World Affairs Journal, and other publications. Her article "Let One Hundred Flowers Be Crushed," about visiting dissidents in China, appeared in the Weekly Standard (December 31, 2007). She has testified before the Senate Foreign Relations Committee and the Congressional-Executive Commission on China. Ms. Bork graduated from Yale University and Georgetown University Law Center.

○